Learn Ruby Programming by Examples

Zhimin Zhan and Courtney Zhan

Learn Ruby Programming by Examples

Zhimin Zhan and Courtney Zhan

ISBN 978-1-50-588288-9

Contents

Preface

On December 8, 2013, US President Barack Obama "asked every American to give it a shot to learn to code" (watch it here[1]), kicking off the Hour of Code campaign for Computer Science Education Week 2013. "Learning these skills isn't just important for your future, it's important for our country's future," President Obama said.

In February 2013, Mark Zuckerberg and Bill Gates and several other big names in IT want kids to learn code (video[2]). I particularly like the quote at the beginning of the video:

> **"Everybody in this country should learn how to program a computer... because it teaches you how to think."** - Steve Jobs

You don't have to be an American to get the message: coding (aka. programming) is an important skill for this information age. Besides the importance of programming, the other message those VIPs also tried to convey is that "you can do it".

As a programmer and software test automation coach, I have worked a lot with manual testers. Manual testing can be repetitive and boring. However, automated testing (using test scripts to drive software applications) is a fun, creative and satisfying job. Writing automated test scripts requires programming skills.

When I introduced the idea of automated test scripts to manual testers, I could immediately sense their fear: "*programming is too hard for me*". This reaction is very typical and common. Don't let the "too hard" phrase discourage you from learning. Let me tell you, programming is not that hard, and it is fun.

Learning programming is a way to master communication with computers, by giving them instructions to perform tasks for you. A programming language is a language that is used to write instructions for computers to understand and execute. There are several popular programming languages such as Java, C#, Ruby, and PHP. For beginners, don't fixate on one. Computers internally work the same way, mastering thinking in programming is more

---

[1] https://www.adafruit.com/blog/2013/12/09/president-obama-calls-on-every-american-to-learn-code/
[2] http://www.psfk.com/2013/02/mark-zuckerberg-bill-gates-coding-school.html

important than one language syntax. In my opinion, different programming languages are like dialects. I learned and taught myself over a dozen of programming languages. Once you have mastered one, it is easy to learn another.

In this book, I will use Ruby, a popular and elegant programming language. Ruby is widely used in enterprise business applications and software testing (*Twitter was initially developed in Ruby*). The main reason I chose Ruby is that it is concise. Therefore, learners can focus more on thinking rather than the syntax.

The most valuable programming skills to have on re-sume

According to the job research data, compiled from thousands of American job ads, by Buring Glass with Brookings Institution economist Jonathan Rothwell in July 2014, Ruby on Rails is the most valuable programming skills with average salary of $109,460[a]. Also, according to Mashable's findings from the CyberCoders database of hundreds of thousands of job postings, Ruby on Rails Developer is the one of top 5 lucrative tech careers to pursue in 2015[b].

[a]http://qz.com/298635/these-programming-languages-will-earn-you-the-most-money
[b]http://mashable.com/2015/02/22/highest-paid-tech-jobs-2015/

I motivated my 13-year old daughter Courtney to learn programming with this book (with the help of President Obama's video). She is the first reader of this book. In fact, I included her thoughts and questions in this book, as well as some of her finished code for the exercises. I think the mistakes Courtney made and the hurdles she faced could be helpful to others. Courtney also designed the book cover and cute illustrations for all the questions, which entitled her the co-author of this book.

What is unique about this book?

A typical how-to-program book will go through the programming concepts, syntax and followed by demonstrations with simple examples. I have read dozens of them (for different programming languages or tools) before and have taught this way at universities. It was not an effective approach. It is more like a teacher dumping knowledge upon students. But I did not know a better way, until I discovered The Michel Thomas Method[3].

---

[3]http://www.michelthomas.com/

The Michel Thomas Method is developed by Michel Thomas for teaching foreign languages. Thomas claimed that his students could "achieve in three days what is not achieved in two to three years at any college". My understanding of this method is that the teacher starts with a simple conversation scenario, then gradually expands the scenario with a few new words each time. That way, students are familiar with the conversation topic and the majority of words or sentences, while learning some new, in real interesting conversations.

I believe this teaching method can be applied to programming. Not only a programming language may also be considered as 'a language', but also very practical. The 'conversation' in speaking languages are exercises in programming. People learn better when they get satisfaction or feedbacks and see their programs running.

As I said before, thinking in programming is much more important than being familiar with a programming language. There is no better way than writing real programs for practical exercises. In this book, I have chosen the exercises that are very simple to understand, besides teaching values, they are useful and fun to do.

Besides programming tutorial books, there are also programming quiz books. I often find some of those exercises are long and hard to understand. Quite commonly, the authors seem to be fond of showing off their programming skills or smart solutions. It won't be the case in this book. This book is a guide to programming and its purpose is to teach. After you finish all the exercises, you will be able to write working programs, and with confidence to continue to learn and grow.

In Chapter 11 (Automation), I will show what you have learnt may lead you to a promising career: test automation engineer for web applications. Web applications are the main stream nowadays. Due to its nature of rapid changes and multi-browser support, automated testing is on demand. However, very few possess the skill. Programming + Automated Testing skills are highly valued in software companies like Facebook: "All Facebook engineers are responsible for writing automated tests for their code"[4].

Who should read this book

Everyone, for whatever reasons: job needs, career change, writing apps or games, or simply to better understand how a computer program works.

In particular, I would strongly encourage young people to give it a go.

---

[4]http://www.theinquirer.net/inquirer/news/1720797/facebook-qa-team

How to read this book

It is highly recommended to read this book from page to page. The exercises are organized into chapters, exercises within each chapter generally follows an easy-to-hard pattern.

The solutions for all exercises are also available on the book's website[5], refer to Resources for access.

Send me feedback

We'd appreciate your comments, suggestions, reports on errors in the book and code. You may submit your feedback on the book's site.

Zhimin Zhan and *Courtney Zhan*

November 2014

---

[5]http://zhimin.com/books/learn-ruby-programming-by-examples

1. Introduction

I still remember my first programming lesson. The first sentence the coach said was "computers are not mysterious". Nobody uses the term 'mysterious' to describe computers nowadays. It was the case in 1980's, computers were rare back then.

We are in the "Information Age" now, computers are a large part of our lives. It seems to me that programming remains mysterious and difficult to the majority of people despite the fact that they spend most of their working hours in front of computers.

Once you have mastered programming, there are many things you can do, such as:

- Instantly rename hundreds of file with a script instead of doing it one by one
- Generate a nice Excel report from raw data instead of typing it in
- Write a document once and use scripts to generate several different formats: HTML (online) and PDF
- Turn on or off certain electronic devices when a certain condition is met
- Write a cool iOS or Android App
- Develop a web application

The bottom line is that when you know how software works you will definitely use computers better.

Before we start, just like my coach, I am telling you that "programming is not mysterious" and you can master it. I believe this book can guide you to the wonderful programming world.

Like many skills, you cannot master programming by reading the book only, you need to **do it**. Let's begin.

1.1 Ruby on Windows

First, we need install Ruby. Download the Ruby Installer for Windows[1] (the latest version to date is Ruby 2.1.3) and run it. Tick the 'Add Ruby executables to your PATH' checkbox on the installation dialog window (accept the defaults for the rest).

---

[1]http://rubyinstaller.org/downloads

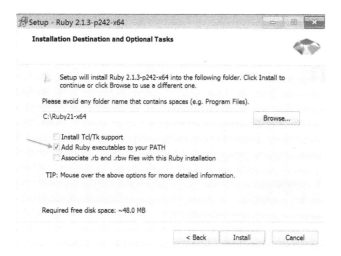

Open command line

The best way to interact with your programs is from the command line. You might have seen these scenes in some Hollywood movies: a hacker types some commands in a window, and something (usually big) happens. The windows that accept user commands (without using a mouse) are called consoles or command windows. To start a command prompt on Windows platform, press 'Start' → 'All Programs' → 'Accessories' → 'Command Prompt'.

You will see a new window like the below.

Type 'ruby -v' in this black window, then press Enter key

If you get the output like the above, that means the Ruby is installed successfully, and is ready to use.

Choose a Ruby Editor

Text Editor is a tool for editing texts (e.g. NotePad). As all the code is in text format, we may use NotePad to write our code in, however, that would not be effective. I recommend the free code editors below:

- Visual Studio Code[2]. A powerful programmer's editor from Microsoft, free.
- SciTE[3]. A free and lightweight programmer's editor. There are several different packages, the easiest one is probably the windows installer (scite-4.0.0x64.msi around 3.2MB).

Write your first Ruby program

I suggest creating a dedicated folder to put all your code in, for example, `C:\Users\you\rubycode`.

Open your editor (I use the free SciTE for illustration), and type in `puts "Hello World!"`. `puts` writes the followed text to the screen.

---

[2]https://code.visualstudio.com/
[3]http://www.scintilla.org/SciTE.html

Save the file to `C:\Users\you\rubycode\helloworld.rb`

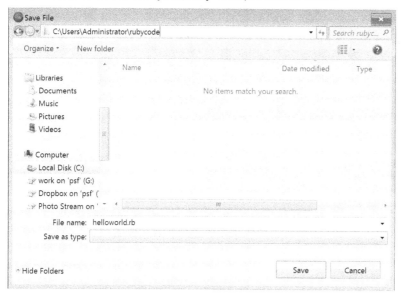

Execution

To run our program, open a command prompt and change the directory to the `rubycode` folder. Type in the command `ruby helloworld.rb`.

```
> cd rubycode
> ruby helloworld.rb
```

```
C:\Users\Administrator>cd rubycode
C:\Users\Administrator\rubycode>ruby helloworld.rb
Hello World
```

1.2 Ruby on Mac OS X

No installation is required as Ruby comes with Mac OS X.

Open command line

The application to access the command line in Mac OS X is called 'Terminal'. Open in Finder: 'Applications' → 'Utilities' → 'Terminal'.

It looks like this:

```
zhimin — bash — 80×24
Last login: Sat Oct 11 14:52:49 on ttys001
MacBook:~ zhimin$
```

Type 'ruby -v', then press Enter key

```
MacBook:~ zhimin$ ruby -v
ruby 2.1.3p242 (2014-09-19 revision 47630) [x86_64-darwin13.0]
```

The ruby version number might be different on your machine, this won't matter.

Choose a Ruby Editor

Commercial

- TextMate[4]. It's was called 'the editor of Mac' and won the Apple Design Award for best developer tool in 2006. It is very popular among Ruby programmers. Cost: €39.

Free

- Visual Studio Code[5].

- TextWrangler[6].

---

[4]http://macromates.com/
[5]https://code.visualstudio.com/
[6]http://www.barebones.com/products/textwrangler/

Write your first Ruby program

I suggest creating a dedicated folder to put all your code in, for example, /Users/YOURUSER-NAME/rubycode.

Start your editor, I would recommend TextMate, but for now (before you decide to purchase TextMate) I would use the free alternative TextWrangler. Open TextWrangler and type in puts "Hello World!". puts writes the followed text to the screen.

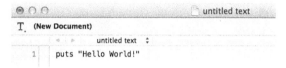

Save to the folder rubycode with the name 'helloworld.rb'

After saving, you will notice that text color changed. This is called Syntax Highlighting. The editor now knows that it is a Ruby program (by the extension *.rb*) and highlights the code accordingly. This will make code much easier to read and identify problems.

Execution

To run our program. Open a Terminal and change the directory to the rubycode folder. Type in the command ruby helloworld.rb.

```
$ cd rubycode
$ ruby helloworld.rb
```

(cd *means 'change directory';* ruby filename *means running this ruby file.*)

You will see the output:

```
Hello World!
```

1.3 Online Ruby Tutorials

While I believe you can learn basic Ruby programming with this book, there are online tutorials that you may use as supplements. For example, read them on your iPad while waiting at bus stops. Here are two good (and free) ones.

Ruby in Twenty Minutes

Ruby in Twenty Minutes[7] is the official Ruby tutorial. As its name suggests, it takes only about 20 minutes to go through.

Codecademy's "Introduction to Ruby" course

Codecademy[8] is a website offers free interactive coding courses. One of them is "Introduction to Ruby". Besides explaining concepts, the course also has simple exercises that you can edit and submit code.

 Why bother this book if I can learn from online Ruby tutorials?

Online tutorials teach you the basic Ruby syntax and some programming concepts. While they are important, these knowledge is only useful if put into practice. For example, to be a good chess player, knowing chess rules is not enough. Though Courtney completed the Codecademy's ruby course first, she has experienced difficulties in doing even the basic programming exercises.

Programming, in my opinion, is a problem solving skill to solve problems in a computer friendly way. This knowledge can only gained by practically coding, which is what this book for. Online tutorials, especially video tutorials, put learners in a passive mode. You need a book such as this one to turn passive knowledge to your own.

1.4 Rhythm for Working on the exercises

Every exercise has 5 sections:

---

[7]https://www.ruby-lang.org/en/documentation/quickstart
[8]http://www.codecademy.com

- **The problem to solve**. It usually comes with sample output for easier understanding. Make sure you understand it well.

- **Purpose**. What you can learn from this exercise.

- **Analyse**. Analyze a problem like a programmer. This is an important step. Quite often we know how to do it but cannot describe it well. Take number sorting as an example; you can sort 5 numbers instantly on top of your head. But how about 100 numbers? This requires you to translate your understanding of sorting step by step into procedures that a computer can execute.

Now **write the code for the exercise**. No one can learn programming by reading, you have to actually do it. You may refer to the hints section to to help you get through.

- **Hints**. I list the hints (in Ruby code format) that may help you to solve the problem when you get stuck.

If you are struggling to solve an exercise, feel free to check out our solutions (at Appendix II). The exercises are selected to introduce new programming skills/practices as well as previous knowledge. So don't worry if you cannot get it right the first time, you will have chances to apply in later exercises. As long as you are trying, you are learning.

- **Solution(s)**. Solutions (can be found at Appendix II) to the most of exercises are between 10 to 20 lines of code. I may show Courtney's solution first with her comments. The runnable solution scripts can be downloaded at the book site.

- **Review**. Think about what you have learnt.

1.5 Suggestions on Windows Layouts

To make it easier for you to write and run your code, I suggest you opening 3 windows as below:

- Code Editor on the left, where you edit the code. (I used free SciTE in the screenshot below).

- A Window explorer with the `rubycode` folder opened.

- A Command Prompt (or Terminal on Mac or Linux) window with current directory is set to `rubycode` folder (execute the command `cd c:\Users\you\rubycode`)

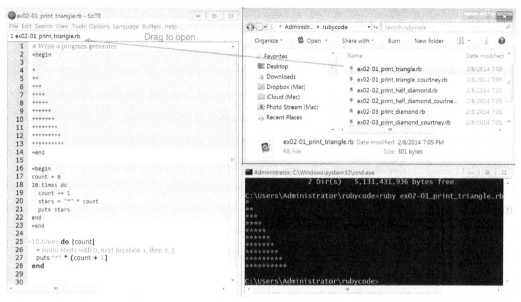

Here are the steps to write and run a new program (*new_code.rb*).

1. In Window Explorer window, right click and create a new text file and rename it to `new_code.rb`. It is important to change the file extension to '.rb'. On Windows, the file extension is hidden in Windows Explorer by default. To change a file extension in Window Explorer, we need to change this setting (to show file extension). Here are the steps for Windows 7.

   - In a Window Explorer window, select 'Organize' → 'Folder and search options'

   - Under 'View' tab, uncheck the "Hide extensions for known file types" checkbox

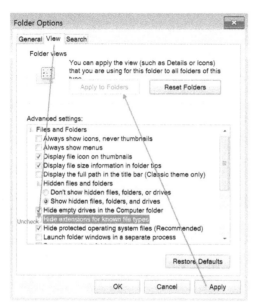

- Click 'Apply' button
- To make it as the default settings (recommended), click 'Apply to Folders' button.

2. Drag the *new_code.rb* file to the editor.

3. Type and edit the code in the editor. Save when it is ready to run.

4. In Command Prompt window, type

```
ruby new_code.rb
```

then press Enter key to run the program.

A quicker way to rerun the program is pressing the 'Up Arrow' key to get the last command.

5. If necessary, repeat Step 3 and 4 until you are satisfied with the result.

1.6 Type of errors

Programmers (new or experienced) encounter code errors every day. I don't expect you to get the exercises right on the first go. We learn from mistakes.

Syntax Error

Ruby checks the syntax of code before running it. If there are syntax errors in code, the error messages are usually quite helpful for identifying the error.

Typo

It is normal that we make typing mistakes when writing code. For example, in the code below, instead 'else' at line 23, I typed `elwe`.

```
21   if row < 8
22       star_count = row + 1
23   elwe
24       star_count = (15 - row)
25   end
```

When I ran the program, I got the error message:

```
ex02-02_print_half_diamond.rb:23:in `block in <main>': undefined local variable or method\
  `elwe' for main:Object (NameError)
from ex02-02_print_half_diamond.rb:20:in `times'
from ex02-02_print_half_diamond.rb:20:in `<main>'
```

The error message means `elwe` is undefined (don't worry if this does not make sense, you will soon understand). The more helpful part in the error trace is the line number 23 (the first line number next to your code file) . It helps identify where the error is.

No matching parenthesis or brackets

Just like Math, if there is a left bracket "(" in code, there shall be a matching right bracket ")". There are also matching keywords for certain code structures, such as `if ... end`. For example, there are two errors in the code below.

```
20   15.times do |row|
21   if row < 8
22       star_count = row + 1        missing ')'
23   else
24       star_count = (15 - row
25                      Missing matching 'end
26   puts '*' * star_count
27   end
```

1. at line 24: missing ')', shall be (15 - row).

2. at line 25: missing `end` for `if` at line 21.

When you run the program, the error message *"expecting ')'"* is correct.

```
ex02-02_print_half_diamond.rb:27: syntax error, unexpected keyword_end, expecting ')'
```

However, the line number 27 is not where the actual error is. That is because it is not possible for Ruby to detect all error scenarios. If the right bracket is on the next line, the program is valid. Only after line 27, Ruby detects the right bracket is actually missing.

After fixing the first error and rerunning the program, a second error occurs. Again, the error line number is not exactly where the real error is.

```
ex02-02_print_half_diamond.rb:27: syntax error, unexpected $end, expecting keyword_end
```

Adding end to line 25 will fix the code.

Runtime error

A runtime error is a software problem that prevents a program from working correctly. When a runtime error occurs, the execution of the program terminates with error messages displayed.

```
a = 5
puts("OK so far")
b = 200 / (a  - 5)
```

The above code runs with an error thrown at line 3, here is the output.

```
OK so far
runtime_error.rb:3:in `/': divided by 0 (ZeroDivisionError)
divided by 0 (ZeroDivisionError)
```

Code logic error

The above two kinds of errors are relatively easy to spot. The difficult errors for programmers are code logic errors. That is, the code can run without syntax errors, but does not behave as it is supposed to. Here is an example.

```
# score below 60 fails the subject
score = read_user_score()
if score > 60
  puts "Pass"
else
  puts "Fail"
end
```

The above code reads a user's exam score and gives the grade: "Pass" or "Fail". It runs fine, most of time, except when the score is 60. There is a code logic error on line 3, it shall be `if score >= 60`.

The ability to debug code errors (find and fix them) separates good programmers from the average. With practice, you will get better on this.

For beginners, I have two practical tips.

1. **One step at a time**. Write one line of code, run the code immediately. This may sound uninteresting, but in practice, many find it is the most useful tip to learn programming. If newly added or changed code fragment caused the error, a click of 'Undo' button (in your editor) will get back your code to previous working state.

2. **If feeling confused, restart**. If you stuck with existing code, chances are the complexity of the code is beyond your control. Try guessing around to get computers to work as instructed (by your code) is highly unlikely. In this case, it is better to restart from scratch. For most of exercises in this book, solutions are less than 20 lines of code.

1.7 Interactive Ruby Shell (IRB)

IRB is a tool that allows the execution of Ruby commands with immediate response, which can be very helpful for learning Ruby syntaxes and debugging code errors. IRB comes with Ruby and it is launched from a command line. To run IRB, just run `irb` from a command line window then try ruby code there.

In the screenshot above, the commands in the green boxes are what I entered. The rest were the responses returned from the commands.

In Appendix 1 ('Ruby in Nutshell') I summarized the core Ruby syntax and usage in examples which you can conveniently run in IRB.

2. Printing Shapes

Printing out asterisk characters (*) in shapes is often used as beginner's programming exercises, as they are simple, easy to understand and visually interesting.

2.1 Print out Triangle

Write a program to print out asterisks like the triangle shape below:

```
*
**
***
****
*****
******
*******
```

Purpose

- Develop ability to analyse patterns
- Variables
- Use of looping

Analyse

Row	The number of stars
1	1
2	2
3	3
...	...
n	n

Hints

Print out text.

```
puts '*'
puts "**"
```

 For small ruby code fragments, you can try them out quickly in IRB.

Generate multiple occurrences of the same character. Please note that the star symbol and Math's multiply symbol are the same in programming languages. However, it is quite easy to distinguish: star symbol is quoted like this "*".

```
'$' * 3  # => '$$$'
```

Because Math's times operator '×' is easy to get confused with the letter 'x' in code , * is commonly used as the multiplication operator in most programming languages.

 Code Comment

Comments are annotations used in code for human to read, computers will ignore them. In Ruby, statements after # are comments.

```
# comment: the code below prints out 10 $ signs.
puts '$' * 10
```

Besides writing down your notes in code as comments, you may also comment out some code fragments when you are not sure to remove them yet.

Using a variable to store an integer.

```
star_count = 2
puts '*' * star_count        # => '**'

star_count = star_count + 1    # now star_count => 3
puts '*' * star_count        # => '***'
```

Variables

You can think of a variable is a 'labeled box' in computers to store data, its data can be changed. The naming convention for Ruby variables is in lower case separated b underscores, for example, `my_birth_date`.

Print out the same text multiple times in a loop (fixed number of times)

```
5.times do
  puts '*'
end
```

The do ... end mark the beginning and end of loop respectively,

Working out the solution on your computer

Make sure you understand the *Analyse* and *Hints* parts before you start.

Courtney's version

```
count = 0
10.times do
  count = count + 1
  stars = "*" * count
  puts stars
end
```

2.2 Print out a half diamond

Write a program that prints out half of the diamond shape using asterisks.

```
*
**
***
****
*****
****
***
**
*
```

Purpose

- Decrement count in loops

Analyse

The key to this problem is to determine the number of stars for the corresponding rows.

```
row 1 to  8: the same as row number
row 9 to 15: 16 - row
```

Hints

Control flows using if ... else

Code, in its simplest form, is executed from top to bottom. But if there are if conditions and loops (and later methods and classes), it will change the flow of execution. The conditional expressions (if-then-else statements) run different code statements depending on a boolean condition (true or false).

```
score = 75
if score < 60
  puts("Failed!")
else
  puts("Pass!")
end
```

Output:

```
Pass!
```

If you change the score = 59 and run again, you will get Failed!.

Boolean condition

The statement score < 60 after if is called a boolean condition. Its value can only be either true or false (which are called boolean values).

Common comparison operators in Ruby

==	equal to
!=	not equal to
<	less than
<=	less than or equal to
>	greater than
>=	greater than or equal to

Examples:

```
2 > 1   # => true
2 == 1  # => false  (equal to)
2 != 1  # => true   (not equal to)
2 <= 2  # true
```

Equal sign = and Double equal sign ==

The equal sign (=) is the "assignment operator", it assigns a value to a variable on the left.

```
a = 1 + 2   # assign 3 to a
```

Please note the "assignment operator" is different from the "equality symbol" in Math. For example, the statement below increases the value of a by 1 (*assign a new value to* a) in programming code. The same equation in Math is invalid.

```
a = a + 1   # increment a by 1
```

The double equal signs (==) is a comparison operator, it compares two values for equality (returns `true` if a is equal to b, `false` otherwise).

```
if a == b
  puts "Found a match!"
end
```

Incorrect use of **=** for **==** is one of the most common mistakes in programming[1].

---

[1]http://www.cprogramming.com/tutorial/common.html

Courtney's version

```
count = 0
8.times do
  count += 1            # this is equivalent to count = count + 1
  stars = "*" * count
  puts stars
end
count = 10
8.times do
  count -= 1
  stars = "*" * count
  puts stars
end
```

Courtney's version loops 16 times (8 + 8), but prints out OK (15 lines). This is because when count is decrement to 0, an empty line is printed out instead.

Courtney uses two loops, which is fine and quite logical for beginners.

2.3 Print out diamond shape

Print 7 rows of '*' in a diamond shape as below:

```
   *
  ***
 *****
*******
 *****
  ***
   *
```

Purpose

- Analyze more complex patterns

Analyse

Below are formulas to calculate the number of star; where `row_number` represents the row number and `total_rows` represents the total number of rows,

1. The number of stars for the rows before the middle one is `(row_number - 1) * 2 + 1`.
2. the number of stars for the rows after the middle one is `(total_rows - row_number) * 2 + 1`

Think about the spaces in front of each row, except for the 4th row (the longest middle one).

Hints

Write down the number of spaces and stars for each row.

```
row 1: print 3 spaces + 1 star
row 2: print 2 spaces + 3 stars
row 3: print 1 space  + 5 stars
row 4: print 0 space  + 7 stars
row 5: print 1 space  + 5 stars
row 6: print 2 spaces + 3 stars
row 7: print 3 spaces + 1 star
```

 If you have difficulty, do it step by step. You may try to print out the top triangle first.

Courtney's version

```
space = " "
space_count = 4
7.times do |row|

  if row < 4
    space_count -= 1
    star_count  = row * 2 + 1
    print space * space_count
  else
    space_count += 1
    star_count  = (7 - 1 - row) * 2 + 1
    print space * space_count
  end
  puts '*' * star_count
end
```

 Courtney says:

I was stuck on the number of stars and number of spaces. I had to sit down with dad to work out the math formula. Also, the multiple variables makes it confusing. So remember to name variables properly and meaningfully. If you are stuck, you can print the variable you think may be the problem. This can help you understand what is going on and how to fix it.

Courtney uses variable space to represent a space string, which is a good practice.

2.4 Print big diamond, name your size

Ask the user for the size of diamond (based on the total number of rows) and then print out a diamond shape using asterisks '*'.

```
Enter the maximum number of rows (odd number): 9
        *
       ***
      *****
     *******
    *********
     *******
      *****
       ***
        *
```

Purpose

- Read user's input into a variable
- Convert string to integer
- Use variable use loop times

Analyse

The size of the diamond is not fixed, it depends on the number the user entered. The number the program asks the user to enter is the total number of rows, which can be stored in an variable.

If you divide the diamond into two parts (top and bottom), work out the number of rows for each part.

Hints

Read user's input

```
user_input = gets  # read user input to a string stored in user_input
```

The above gets accepts a line of text from keyboard and assigns the string typed and a "\n" character to variable user_input. "\n" is a new line character, which is added when the user press Enter key. Quite often, we want to remove this "\n" immediately. Here is code to do that:

```
user_input = gets.chomp
```

String and Fixnum

The String and Fixnum (number) are two most common data types in Ruby.

```
a = "12"
b = "3"
a + b        # => "123"

c = 12
d = 3
c + d        # => 15
```

Adding a String to an Fixnum will get an error.

```
a.class  # => String
c.class  # => Fixnum
a + c    # return errors TypeError: no implicit conversion of Fixnum into String
```

Convert a number string to integer

```
"6".to_i        # => to integer 6
"12".to_i  + 3  # => 15
```

Math divide operator in Ruby: "/"

```
 8 / 2                # => 4
 9 / 2                # => 4,  ignore the remainder
 (1 + 2) * 3 + 3 / 2  # => 10
```

Courtney's version

```
puts "Enter the maximum number of rows (odd number):"
size = gets.chomp.to_i
space = " "
space_count = size / 2 + 1

size.times do |row|
  if row < (size / 2 + 1)
    space_count -= 1
    star_count  = row * 2 + 1
    print space * space_count
  else
    space_count += 1
    star_count  = (size - 1 - row) * 2 + 1
    print space * space_count
  end
  puts '*' * star_count
end
```

Courtney says:

When I first tried replacing diamond size with user input variable, I forgot to change the variables and that made the outcome completely different. It is not hard to fix it though.

You must know it first, then instruct computers

Trying to enter a big number for the last program, say 99. It will print a big diamond, Wow!

This an important aspect of programming. Once you figure out the pattern and logic of a problem and translate it into computer understandable language (program), it can solve the similar problems at any scale. For example, the effort taken for computers to calculate 2 x 2 is not much different from 12343 x 35345. In other words, we (human) must understand **how** to solve the problem first. Programming translates the how into instructions that computers can follow.

2.5 Exercises

Write code to print out the shapes below, the width of shape is changeable.

Rhombus

```
    *****
   *****
  *****
 *****
*****
```

Hollow Square

```
*****
*   *
*   *
*   *
*****
```

Heart

```
   *****     *****
  *******   *******
 ********* *********
*******************
 *****************
  ***************
   *************
    ***********
     *********
      *******
       *****
        ***
         *
```

Hints

The first three rows are static regardless of the size.

3. Quiz Time

We will do some computer interaction exercises.

3.1 Simple Add Calculator

 Write a simple calculator that adds two integers (up to 99) from user inputs and prints out the sum.

```
I am an adding machine, and I am good at it.
Enter first number: (type 1, press Enter)
Enter second number: (type 99, press Enter)
Thinking ...
Got it, the answer is: 100
```

Purpose

- Read user's keyboard input
- Use variables for mathematic operations
- Print variable in a string

Analyse

An adding operation requires two inputs which we need to collect from the user. The user-inputted number must be stored (in variables) before we can add them up and output the sum.

Hints

Read user's keyboard input

```
gets.chomp  # read user input, end with Enter key
"123".to_i  # convert string to integer
```

Print variables in string

```
name = "Courtney"
age  = 13
puts "My name is " + name   # OK
puts "My age is " + age     # Error!
puts "My age is " + age.to_s    # OK
```

The second puts statement will throw an error TypeError: no implicit conversion of Fixnum into String. This is because Ruby detects "a string plus an integer (age)".

One way to overcome this problem is to embed the variables within a double quoted string using #{variable}.

```
name = "Courtney"
age  = 13
puts("Hello, My name is #{name}, I am #{age} years old.")
```

Output:

```
Hello, My name is Courtney, I am 13 years old.
```

3.2 Addition Quiz

 Write a program to prompt 10 single digit addition questions, provide feedback based on user's response and then print out the score.

```
1 + 1 =  (enter 2)
Correct.
2 + 7 = (enter 8)
Wrong!
...
6 + 3 =

Your score: 8/10
```

Purpose

- Use rand() to generate a random number
- Looping
- Incrementing a variable (counting)

Analyse

10 questions means repeating the following operations 10 times

1. generate one number
2. generate another number
3. ask user for the answer
4. check the answer and print out feedback

To get a score, you will need to prepare a counter. If the user's input is correct, increment the counter by 1.

Hints

Generate a random number

A random number is a computer generated number in a nondeterministic manner. Random numbers are quite useful for a variety of purposes, such as simulation in games, encryption, quiz (like this exercise), etc. To generate a random number within a range:

```
rand(10) # a random number between 0 to 9
```

The generated random number will be different for each run.

Counting

Incrementing the variable by 1.

```
count = 0 # clear it first
5.times do
  count = count + 1
end
puts count # => 5
```

Stop program

Press Ctrl+C to terminate the program's execution.

3.3 Subtraction Quiz

 Write a program to prompt 10 single digit subtraction questions, provide feedback based on user's response and then print out the score.

```
9 - 1 =  (enter 8)
Correct.
7 - 2 = (enter 8)
Wrong!
...
Your score: 8/10
```

Purpose

- Use logic control (if)
- Be consistent with changes: changing a part code here might affect there.

Analyse

It might seem like the previous exercise, however, this one can be a little tricky.

Hints

Subtraction in this context is using a bigger number to minus a smaller number. The random number generator does not guarantee the first number is bigger.

Courtney's version

```
count = 0
10.times do
  num1 = rand(10)
  num2 = rand(10)
  if num1 > num2
    print "#{num1} - #{num2} = "
    answer = num1 - num2
  else
    print "#{num2} - #{num1} = "
    answer = num2 - num1
  end
  input = gets.chomp.to_i
  if answer == input
    puts "Correct!"
    count += 1
  else
    puts "Wrong!"
  end
end
puts "Your score is #{count}/10"
```

 Courtney says:

I didn't get it right first time as I forgot to change the answer. If you want to change one thing you may have to change others because they affect each other.

Her initial (incorrect) version was:

```
if num1 > num2
  print "#{num1} - #{num2} = "
else
  print "#{num2} - #{num1} = "
end
answer = num1 - num2
```

This caused some confusion, where the answer was not matching the question. Because the two numbers are randomly generated and the answer is only correct when the first number is bigger, otherwise the answer will be a negative number. This kind of errors in programming are called **intermittent errors**, which are hard to discover.

Also, the count increment statement works but is not in a good format.

```
count = count += 1 # bad way
count += 1          # OK
count  = count + 1 # OK too
```

3.4 Number Guessing Game

 The computer has a secret number (0 to 9), the program prompts the user to enter a guess and give feedback such as 'too big' or 'too small'. The program ends when a correct answer is entered.

```
I have a secret number (0 - 9), Can you guess it?
=> (you type 9)
Too big!
=> (you type 4)
Too Small!
=> (you type 5)
Correct! You guessed 3 times.
```

Purpose

- Infinity looping
- Exit program or looping

Analyse

Different from the previous exercises, the number of times the computer 'prompts' is nondeterministic. The program ends when the player answered correctly.

Hints

Infinity loop

An infinity loop is a sequence of code loops endlessly.

```
while true
  # ...
end
```

The Apple Campus is the corporate headquarters of Apple Inc., located at 1 Infinite Loop in Cupertino, California, United States. (source Wikipedia[1])

Exit from a loop

Obviously we need an exit mechanism to make infinity loop useful.

```
# ...
  break        # ends the current loop
# ...
```

or quit the program completely.

```
exit
```

For example,

```
while true {
  # ... calculate result
  if result > 60 {
    puts("You passed")
    break
  }
}
puts "made here"
```

---

[1]http://en.wikipedia.org/wiki/Infinite_Loop_%28street%29

Courtney's version

```
puts "I have a secret number (0-9) Can you guess it?"
count = 0
input = nil    # nil means no value
answer = rand(10)
until input == answer
  input = gets.chomp.to_i
  count += 1
  if input > answer
    puts "TOO BIG"
  elsif input < answer
    puts "too small"
  else
    puts "CORRECT"
  end
end
puts " The number is : #{answer}. and you guessed #{count} times!!"
```

 Courtney says:

I had trouble with this one. I had two inputs which made one of them work and
the other not. I had also confused the loop with the if and that changed the whole
thing.

Courtney actually got stuck, probably due to doing it in a rush (so she could play her video
game). After I asked her to restart from scratch, she got it right.

Here is what she meant "two inputs":

```
input = gets.chomp.to_i
until input == answer
  input = gets.chomp.to_i
  # ...
end
```

The first input = gets.chomp.to_i is what she used to have at the beginning of program
(a habit). Then she realized that the program needs to ask for the user's input again,
therefore she added the second input = gets.chomp.to_i in the loop. The program
reads an unnecessary user input, which confused her. Removing the first line input =
gets.chomp.to_i got the following error:

```
undefined local variable or method `input'
```

Not wanting to change her code, I hinted that the `input` variable can be set to nil at the beginning.

```
input = nil   # nil means no value
# ...
```

Courtney used `until` instead the infinity looping `while` (suggested in the hint), which is fine.

3.5 Exercises

Counting to 21

You and computer each take turns counting to 21, whoever say 21 loses.

Hangman

Write a program to guess a word by trying to guess the individual characters. The word to be guessed shall be provided using the command-line argument.

Your program shall look like:

```
My secret word: _____

Key in one character or the guess word: a
Try 1: _____a__
Key in one character or the guess word: t
Try 2: ___t_a__
Key in one character or guess word: o
Try 3: _oot_a__
Key in one character or the guess word: football
Try 4: Correct!
You got it in 4 tries.
```

Hints

If you are not familiar with Array, come to to do this exercise after the next chapter.

4. Array and Hash

In previous exercises, we used simple data types such as Strings and Integers (called Fixnum prior to Ruby 2.4). There are composite data types that are a collection of other types. The most common composite data types are Array and Hash. An array is like a list and a hash is like a dictionary-like lookup.

In this chapter, we will write some programs using Array and Hash. The Ruby official documentation has good explanation on them and all their methods are listed, even with easy to understand examples.

- Ruby Array Doc[1]
- Ruby Hash Doc[2]

4.1 Sort Children Names

Names A..Z

Ask a list of names and then output them in alphabetical order. The program ends when the user enters "0".

```
Enter child names in class: (0 to finish):
Dominic
Courtney
Anna
Angela
Ella
Toby
Emma
0

Kids in order:
Angela, Anna, Courtney, Dominic, Ella, Emma, Toby
```

---

[1]http://www.ruby-doc.org/core-2.4.0/Array.html
[2]http://www.ruby-doc.org/core-2.4.0/Hash.html

Purpose

- Adding data into an array
- Array sorting
- End a loop on a condition
- Display array

Analyse

There are two steps: collecting names and sorting them.

Hints

Add an element to an array

An array is a sequence of data.

```
aus_states = []      # initialize an empty array
aus_states = ["NSW", "VIC"]   # initialize an array with data
aus_states << "QLD" # aus_states now ["NSW", "VIC", "QLD"]
```

Sorting an array

```
array = ["Google", "Apple", "Sony", "Samsung"] # define an array
# will sort array in ascending order
array.sort # => ["Apple", "Google", "Samsung", "Sony"]
array.join(", ") # => "Google, Apple, Samsung, Sony"
array.sort.join(", ") # => "Apple, Google, Samsung, Sony"
```

Please note `array.sort` returns the array's elements in sorted order, but no changes to the array itself.

 You have done collecting multiple user inputs in "Guessing Number" exercise in last chapter. If you have trouble with this exercise, starting from there.

1. Collecting names from user input
2. Add names (one by one) to an array
3. Print out sorted elements (in an array)

4.2 Get the character from given alphabetical position

A 1   Asks the user to enter a number between 1 to 26, and then print the character at the alphabetical position. The program ends when the user enters "0".

```
I know the alphabet very well, enter the alphabetical order number (integer) and I will t\
ell you the corresponding letter, 0 to quit:
1 (user enter)
is 'A'
5 (user enter)
is 'E'
0
Bye!
```

Purpose

- Access array element by index
- Infinite loop with exit condition

Analyse

The number of times the user can input is undetermined. So it will be an infinite loop with an exit condition: when '0' is entered.

We can use the alphabet position to look up in a predefined array for the corresponding character.

Hints

Like many programming languages, array indexing starts with **0**, not 1.

```
array = ["Google", "Apple", "Sony", "Samsung"]
# accessing elements in this array
array[0]  # => "Google"
array[2]  # => "Sony"
array[-1] # => "Samsung"
```

4.3 Calculate Average

Ask the user to enter a set of student scores (non-negative) integers and then calculate the average. The program ends when the user enters "-1".

```
Enter scores: (enter -1 to finish):
87
94
100
56
74
67
75
88
-1

Average score : 80
```

Analyse

Calculation of the average is easy (see the hints below) by using existing Ruby's array functions.

Purpose

- Add data element into an array
- Sum an array

Hints

Try to do the sum first and then calculate the average. There are two ways to sum all elements in array:

```
# adding all elements in an array: classic way
array = [1, 2, 3]
the_sum = 0
array.each do |num|
  the_sum += num
end
```

The standard and more concise way to sum an array of numbers.

```
the_sum = array.inject{|sum,x| sum + x }
```

Courtney's version

```
array = []
count = 0
puts "Enter scores: "
while true
  input = gets.chomp.to_i
  if input == -1
    break
  else
    array << input
    count += 1
  end
end
sum = 0
array.each do |number|
  sum += number
end
average = sum / count

puts "Average score: #{average}"
```

4.4 What makes 100% in life?

X = Life 100%?

If we represent the alphabet numerically by identifying sequence of letters (A,B,C,...,X,Y,Z) with the percentages (1%,2%,3%,...,24%,25%,26%). A sum of each characters' value in a word is the meaning to life percentage. Then

H-A-R-D-W-O-R-K = $(8+1+18+4+23+15+18+11)\% = 98\%$

Ask user to enter an English word (or string) and calculate its meaning to life percentage.

```
Enter your word (in capital): HARDWORK
The value of meaning to life: 98%
```

Try the words: "KNOWLEDGE", "ATTITUDE", "VIDEOGAME"

Purpose

- Use of Hash for looking up
- Treat string as an array

Analyse

Three main steps:

1. Break up a string into a list of characters
2. For each character, find out its percentage value (integer).
3. Add all the percentage values up

Hints

Looping each character in a string

```
"ABC".split("").each do |ch|
  # process ch as a character
end
```

Get the value from a hash by a given key

```
# define a Hash
cities_abbrevs = { "LA" => "Los Angeles", "NY" => "New York" }

# look up in a Hash
cities_abbrevs["NY"] # => "New York"
cities_abbrevs["SF"] # => nil, no entry matching the key "SF"
```

Here is another Hash example: data type of keys and values are different (*string* ⇒ *integer*).

```
numbers = { "one" => 1, "two" => 2 }
numbers["one"] + numbers["two"]  # =>  3
```

Courtney's version

```
array = []
hash = {  "A" => 1,"B" => 2,"C" => 3, "D" => 4, "E" => 5, "F" => 6, "G" => 7, "H" => 8, "\
I" => 9, "J" => 10, "K" => 11, "L" => 12, "M" => 13, "N" => 14, "O" => 15, "P" => 16, "Q"\
 => 17, "R" => 18, "S" => 19, "T" => 20, "U" => 21, "V" => 22, "W" => 23, "X" => 24,"Y" =\
> 25, "Z" => 26}
puts "Enter word in capitals"
input = gets.chomp

input.split("").each do |character|
  array << hash[character]
end

the_sum = array.inject{|sum,x| sum + x}
puts "The value of meaning to life: #{the_sum}%"
```

 Courtney says:

I found this one very difficult. After the users input is added, the loops make it harder and I didn't realize that I needed to use the array until later. I also found the hashes difficult and hard to use. Hashes are used to look up a key to find the value (key ⇒ value). Sometimes it helps to write what you are going to do on paper then work it out using ruby.

Courtney got stuck here. After some hints and explanation, especially showing how to do it manually on paper, she managed to get it done; but it took quite long time (45 minutes).

4.5 Exercises

Find the Median

The Median is the "middle" of a sorted list of numbers. For example, the median of the data set 1, 1, 2, **5**, 6, 6, 9 is 5. If there is an even number of data values the median is the mean of the two data values in the middle. For example, the median of the data set 4, 2, 1, 3, 5, 4 is 3. It is the mean of *3* and *4* or, (3 + 4) /2 = 3.5.

Write a program to find the median of a list of numbers. The output shall be like this:

```
Enter a list of numbers (separated by space): 4 2 1 3 5 4
The Median is:  3.5
```

Hints

Split a string of list numbers to an integer array

```
"12 15 7 8 25".split.collect{|x| x.to_i }  # => [12, 15, 7, 8, 25]
```

5. Useful Utility Programs

In this chapter, we will write some utility program that you might find useful.

5.1 Fahrenheit to Celsius Converter

Julie, an Australian, is going to USA, where different Fahrenheit temperature scales are used. Here is the Fahrenheit to Celsius formula: $T_c = \frac{5}{9}(T_f - 32)$.

Can you write a program for Julie to convert Fahrenheit to Celsius? The result is rounded to 2 digits after the decimal point.

```
Enter temperature in Fahrenheit: 100.5
In Celsius: 38.06
```

Purpose

- Apply math formula into programming
- Float number
- Rounding

Analyse

This is just simple calculation based on a given formula. So far our calculations are using integers only. This one has floating numbers, which are decimal numbers.

Hints

Convert a string to a float number

```
"34.123".to_f
```

In Ruby, the result of dividing two integers is also an integer.

```
100 / 3  # => 33
```

To get more precise result.

```
100.0 / 3  # => 33.3333333

# when variables used
a = 100
a * 1.0 /3
```

Rounding.

```
37.455.round(2)   # => 37.46
```

Courtney says:

I initially used the `inputs= gets.chomp.to_i` at first, the output was 37.0 instead of 37.46. I tried printing out the input after entering 100.5 (for debugging), the number returned was 100! Changing `to_i` to `to_f` corrected it.

5.2 Personal Income Tax Calculator

 Here are Australian personal income tax rates for 2016-17 financial year.

Taxable income	Tax on this income
0 – $18,200	Nil
$18,201 – $37,000	19c for each $1 over $18,200
$37,001 – $80,000	$3,572 plus 32.5c for each $1 over $37,000
$87,001 – $180,000	$19,822 plus 37c for each $1 over $80,000
$180,001 and over	$54,232 plus 45c for each $1 over $180,000

Write a program to calculate how much tax an Australian needs to pay based on his or her annual salary.

```
Enter your annual income: 80000
Your personal income tax amount: $17547
```

Analyse

The calculation is easy. The key here is to compare the user entered amount against thresholds (note, I used plurals here).

Purpose

- Branching using `if`, `elsif` and `else`
- Logical operators `&&` ("and")
- `case` and `when`

 Complete this exercise using `if`, `else if` and `else` first, then change to `switch` statement. Review the difference.

Hints

IF-ELSE IF

The branching concept is simple and self-explanatory.

```
a  = 10
if a < 10
  puts "single digit"
elsif a >= 100
  puts "too big, I don't know"
else
  puts "two digits"
end
```

The statements after `if` and `elsif` are conditions. Their value can only be either `true` or `false` (which are called boolean values).

Logical operators

&&	AND
||	OR

Example:

```
a = 10
if a > 0 && a < 10
  puts "#{a} is a positive single digit number"
end
```

CASE-WHEN

When dealing with a large number of possible conditions, `case` statement is better than `if-else` in terms of code clarity.

```
score = 70

result = case score
   when 0..60
     "Fail"
   when 61..70
      "Pass"
   when 71..95
     "Pass with Distinction"
   when 96, 97, 98, 99
     "Distinction"
   when 100
     "High Distinction"
   else
     "Invalid Score"
   end
puts result # => Pass
```

5.3 Word count

Emily wrote a book review, but she is not sure whether it meets the required word count. Assuming Emily's article is already saved in a string, can you write a program to count the number of words?

(assuming the text is "'Practical Web Test Automation' book is great. The end.")

```
The text has 9 words.
```

Purpose

- Tokenization, split strings by separators into an array
- Count array size

Analyse

Words are separated by spaces (we will use this rule for the exercise). Counting how many spaces is not a good idea, as two consecutive spaces shall be counted as one in this case.

One way is to use tokenization[1], splitting the text into tokens by whitespace characters.

Hints

Use split method to split a string into an array with a given separator.

```
pixar_movies = "Toy Story,A Bug's Life,Incredibles,Toy Story 2,Finding Nemo,Ratatouille,C\
ars"
pixar_movie_list = pixar_movies.split(",")
pixar_movie_list.size # => 7
pixar_movie_list[0]   # => "Toy Story"
```

If no separator is given, a string is split on white spaces.

---

[1]http://en.wikipedia.org/wiki/Tokenization

```
good_movies = "Toy Story 2,Finding Nemo"
good_movies.split # => ["Toy", "Story", "2,Finding", "Nemo"]
```

 Courtney says:

I found this one rather easy, except I did not name my variables properly and had to rename them.

5.4 Generate Lotto Numbers

 Write a program to generate 6 Lotto numbers. Lotto numbers are between 1 and 49.

```
Your winning lotto numbers are [23, 34, 12, 6, 7, 49], good luck!
```

Purpose

- Check whether an array contains an element
- Use of random number generator

Analyse

Obviously, we need the lotto numbers to be randomly generated, and they have to be unique. We can use rand(). However, the random number generator may generate duplicate ones.

Here is one way. Let's say, you are the picker for the lotto and have six buckets on a table. Each bucket contains 49 individually numbered balls (from 1 to 49).

1. You go to the first bucket, close your eyes, pick up one ball and put on the table.
2. Go to the next bucket, close eyes, pick up another ball.
3. If this number was already on the table, put the ball back to the bucket.
4. Repeat the step 2 again until find the number is not already on the table.
5. Repeat 4 more times, then you get all 6 unique lotto numbers.

Hints

Check whether an array contains one element, i.e. check the uniqueness.

```
array = ["Apple", "Sony"]
array.include?("Apple")   # => true
array.include?("Samsung") # => false
```

5.5 Number sorting

Numbers   Ask the user to input 10 numbers, then sort them in order.

```
Please enter 10 numbers:
10
8
7
3
4
5
9
1
2
6

The numbers in order: 1, 2, 3, 4, 5, 6, 7, 8, 9, 10
```

Note: built-in sorting functions are not allowed.

Analyse

Imagine you have 5 coins with different values: 10c , 20c, 50c, $1, and $2. How do you sort the coins (from small to big)? I know it is obvious to human. But by now, you probably know that we need to translate our solution into steps that computers can understand.

Let's get back to our coin sorting problem. There are 5 coins on the table. You pick up the first coin (from left to right) in your left hand, then compare it to the rest one by one (by picking it up in your right hand). If the one in your left hand is smaller, put back the the coin in your right hand and continue. If the one in your left hand is bigger, swap with the one in your right hand. Basically, after each comparison, make sure the one in your left hand is smaller. After one iteration, the one in your left hand is the smallest. Put this one aside on a cloth, now there shall be 4 coins left on the table. Then starting another iteration, when done, put the coin (in left hand) on the right side of the last coin on the cloth. Repeat until only one coin left. The coins on the cloth are sorted (from small to large).

Pseudocode is a high level description of a computer program. The idea of pseudocode is to convey how the problem shall be solved without being locked with a particular programming language. Here is the pseudocode for the above:

```
for each element in the list
  identify current_one
  for the next one (index) to the last one (index) do
    if any one in remaining is bigger than current_one
      swap them
    end if
  end for (inside)
end for (outside)
```

Purpose

- Iterating an array
- Swapping variables
- Access elements in an array using index
- Looping an array from specific index range

Hints

Swapping variables

To swap two variables, it is traditionally (in most programming languages) done via a third variable:

```
c = a
a = b
b = c
```

This is a common pattern and to help me remember, I used the phrase "ca-ab-bc".

In Ruby, it can be done much neater:

```
a, b = b, a
```

Iterating an array, get the array element by index

```
array.each_with_index do |num, idx|
  # array[idx] to access the current element
end

array[0]                # first one
array[array.size() - 1] # last one
array[-1]               # also last one
```

To loop an array from a specific index range

```
array = ["A", "B", "C", "D", "E", "F", "G"]
(2..(5-1)).each do |an_idx|
  puts array[an_idx]
end
# will print out "C", "D", "E" (the index from 2 to 4)
```

5.6 Exercises

Convert Decimal to Hex

Write a program to convert an input decimal string into its equivalent hexadecimal. Your output shall look like:

```
Decimal number: 398
The equivalent hexadecimal number: 18E
```

Hints

Decimal to Hex

```
428 / 16  # => 26,  remain: 12
 26 / 16  # =>  1,  remain: 10
  1 / 16  # =>  0,  remain:  1
```

Convert the remains of the above based on all hex numbers ['0', '1', '2', '3', '4', '5', '6', '7,' '8', '9', 'A', 'B', 'C', 'D', 'E', 'F'], in reversing order.

```
 1  =>  1
10  =>  A
12  =>  C
```

The hexadecimal for decimal number '428' is '1AC'.

Convert Hex to Decimal

Write a program to convert an input hexadecimal string into its equivalent decimal number. Your output shall look like:

```
Hexadecimal : 1a
The equivalent decimal number for hexadecimal "1a" is 26
```

Hints

Power operator (Math)

```
2 ** 3  # => 8
5 ** 3  # => 125
```

Hex to Decimal

```
# A5BE is a hex number
A5BE = 10 * (16 ** 3) + 5 * (16 ** 2) + 11 * (16 ** 1) + 14 * (16 ** 0)
     = 42430
```

Word to Phone Number Converter

On phone keypad, the alphabets are mapped to digits as follows:

```
         ABC(2)   DEF(3)
GHI(4)   JKL(5)   MNO(6)
PQRS(7)  TUV(8)   WXYZ(9)
```

Write a program thats prompts user for a String (case insensitive), and converts to a sequence of Keypad digits.

```
Enter your PhoneWords: 1800 TESTWISE
The actual phone number: 1800 83789473
```

6. Fun Math

Computers were created originally to do mathematic computation, hence it is named 'computer'. Math is an essential part of software design. I know for many, 'fun' is not the word to describe Math. Programming, in my opinion, can add a 'fun' factor to Math.

There are two-way benefits: programming allows you to understand Math better and you can utilize your Math skills to solve problems.

6.1 Finding Divisors

 Write a program to list all divisors of a given number (user entered).

```
Enter a number: (108)
The divisors of 108: 1, 2, 3, 4, 6, 9, 12, 18, 27, 36, 54, 108
```

Analyse

To determine whether a number is divisible by another, check the remainder of the division. 0 means divisible.

Purpose

- Determine a number is fully divisible.

Hints

Ruby's modulo operator: % returns the remainder of a division.

```
8 % 3 # => 2
9 % 3 # => 0
```

6.2 Finding the Highest Common Factor

Write a program to ask the user to enter two non-negative integers and then find the highest common factor (HCF).

```
Enter the first number: (8)
Enter the second number: (12)
The HCF of 8 and 12 is: 4
```

Highest Common Factor

The largest common factor of two or more numbers is called the highest common factor. The HCF is also known as greatest common devisor (gcd). For example,

```
8 =  1 x 8 = 2 x 4
12 = 1 x 12 = 2 x 6 = 3 x 4
```

So the common factors of 8 and 12 are: 1, 2 and 4 (1, 2, 4 and 8 for 8; 1, 2, 3, 4, 6 and 12 for 12). 4 is the highest common factor.

Purpose

- Iterate an array
- Check whether an element is in an array?
- Use break to terminate a loop

Analyse

There are several methods to compute the HCF. I am going to focus on a simple way. As a matter of fact, this method has the most steps but it is the easiest one to understand.

1. Compute all divisors of the first number and note them down, e.g. 8 => [1, 2, 4, 8]

2. Compute all divisors of the second number and note them down, e.g, `12 => [1, 2, 3, 4, 6, 12]`

3. Find the largest one in both divisors list: Starting with one, work you way down, and check whether the divisor is also in the second. The first divisor found in both divisors list is HCF (*check divisor from large to small*).

Knowing the answer to working out the algorithm

For the above example, Step 3 is quite obvious to human. If I ask you why, many might not be able to answer. Some might say: "It is obvious when seeing two divisor list". However, if the two numbers are 103096 and 234986, it is a different story, isn't it?

Computers are not 'afraid of' big numbers like us, they just need an algorithm in a set of steps to execute. If you know the answer, it means you know the algorithm, but may not be good at expressing it out. This takes time and practice. In my view, mastering this makes you a programmer. The best way is to start with simple examples. Imagine yourself as a computer, then work out steps on a paper.

Hints

Store divisors of each number into two separate arrays.

```
divisors_list_1 = [1, 2, 4, 8]
divisors_list_2 = [1, 2, 4, 8, 12]
```

Sort an array from large to small order.

```
divisors_list_1.sort.reverse # => [8,4,2,1]
```

Iterate (i.e, go through one by one) one array (`divisors_list_1`). For each element in this array (`divisors_list_1`), check whether the other array (`divisors_list_2`) contains the divisor. The first divisor found in both arrays is HCF.

```
array = [1, 2, 3, 6]
array.each do |elem|
  # process the elem.
end
```

```
array = [1, 2, 3, 6]
array.include?(2) # => true
array.include?(7) # => false
```

Courtney's version

Courtney says:

I found this one very hard as I didn't quite understand how to achieve my goal. At first I made my code very confusing and ended up having it deleted and started from scratch. This happened twice. On the first attempt, I was unsure how to get to the HCF and on the second attempt I didn't do the main part of the code. Instead, the outer part (like puts) made it hard to continue. My lesson: must first understand the objective, work on the main part, then do the other bits.

```
divisors_list_1 = []
divisors_list_2 = []
puts "Enter first number: "
num1 = gets.chomp.to_i
(1..num1).each do |x|
    check = num1 % x
    if check == 0
        divisors_list_1 << x
    end
end
puts "Enter second number: "
num2 = gets.chomp.to_i
(1..num2).each do |x|
    check = num2 % x
    divisors_list_2 << x   if check == 0
end

d1sorted = divisors_list_1.sort.reverse
d1sorted.each do |elem|
    # puts "elem = #{elem}"
    if divisors_list_2.include?(elem)
        puts "The HCF is #{elem}"
        break
    end
end
```

6.3 Finding the Least Common Multiple (LCM)

12 18
 \/
  36

Least (also sometimes called Lowest) common multiple is the smallest (non-zero) number that is a multiple of two or more examples. For example, 12 is the LCM of 6 and 4, as 12 = 6 x 2 and 12 = 3 x 4. 24 is also a common multiple of 4 and 6, but is not the lowest.

```
Enter the first number: (6)
Enter the second number: (4)
The LCM for 6 and 12 is: 12
Calculation time: 0.0001 seconds
```

Now, try bigger numbers such as 4254 and 82835.

```
The LCM for 4254 and 82835 is: 352380090
Calculation time: 25.564194 seconds
```

Let's see how you can improve the calculation speed.

Purpose

- Use step for looping
- Timing code execution
- Optimize program performance

Analyse

A simple way is to search the number from the larger one of the two to the multiple of the two. For example,

```
(6..6*4).each do |n|
  # check whether n is LCM?
end
```

The above brute-force way is not optimal. Obviously, it will take longer due to too many looping (a * b) when the two numbers are big.

One of the most effective way to speed up your program is to reduce the number of loops. For this example, it is not necessary to check each number from 6, 7 , 8, 9, 10, 11, 12, ..., 24. We just need to check every multiple of 6, i.e, 6, 12, 18, 24.

Hints

Loop with steps

```
(6..24).step(6) do |n|
  puts n
end
# will print out 6, 12, 18, 24
```

Time the code execution time

```
start_time = Time.now
# ... the code
puts "Calculation took #{Time.now - start_time} seconds"
```

 if the output of the above code like 4.2e-05 seconds, this means the time is too short to be meaningful.

Courtney's version

At first I wrote that the LCM was divisible by num1 OR num2. This was wrong because this made 6 the LCM of 6 and 12. Instead of using or (||), you need to use and (&&).

When working with the lowest number first, it took much longer to generate the LCM. So I had to make the higher number always first, and it was quicker.

```
puts "Enter the first number: "
num1 = gets.chomp.to_i
puts "Enter the second number:"
num2 = gets.chomp.to_i
if num1 > num2
    check = num1
else
    check = num2
end
puts "check = #{check}"
start_time = Time.now
(check..num1 * num2).step(check) do |n|
    #          puts "n % num1 = #{n % num1}"
    #          puts "n % num2 = #{n % num2}"
    if n % num1 == 0 && n % num2 == 0
        puts "The LCM for #{num1} and #{num2} is #{n}"
        break
    end
end
puts "Calculation took #{Time.now - start_time} seconds"
```

6.4 Finding Prime Numbers

 Find prime numbers between 1 and 20.

```
Prime numbers (up to 20) are : 2, 3, 5, 7, 11, 13, 17, 19
```

 ## Prime Number

A prime number is a number that is bigger than one and has no divisors other than 1 and itself. For example, 5 is prime, since no number except 1 and 5 divides it. On the other hand, 6 is not a prime (it is a composite), since 6 = 2 x 3.

Analyse

The below is a pseudocode for finding prime numbers.

Pseudocode

```
for each number x in 2 .. 10
  for x with 2,3,4,5,6,..., x-1 (another loop)
    clear the flag (assuming it is prime number initially)
    if number can be divided by x (remainder is 0)
      oops, it is not a prime number
      mark a flag
      break
    end
  end inner for loop
  if no flag set
    this is a good prime number (it passed our checks)
    print out this prime number
  end
end outer for loop
```

Make sure you completely understand the logic to determine a prime number before coding.

Purpose

- Ranges in Ruby
- Use a flag variable to store a status

Hints

Ruby Range is a set of values within a specified begin and end. For example, (1..4) contains 1, 2, 3 and 4.

```
(2..5).each do |x|
  puts x
end
# will print 2, 3, 4, 5 in four lines.

# convert a range to an array
2..5.to_a  # => [2, 3, 4, 5]
```

Set a flag within a loop, and check it later

This is a common and very useful programming practice.

```
is_composite = false
[2,3,4,5,6,7].each do |num|
  if 8 % num == 0
    is_composite = true
    break
  end
end
if is_composite
  puts "8 is a composite number"
end
```

In above code, the variable `is_composite` is a flag. It was initially set to `false` and its value may be changed by the following computation code. So later we can use its value to determine the prime numbers.

Courtney's version

Courtney struggled with it. I thought due to the following reasons:

- Courtney learned prime numbers a few year ago in grade 4. However I don't think her understanding of prime numbers is good enough to program.
- I didn't include the hint of using flag (kind of my fault, now added)
- While she understands the ruby ranges and check divisible by using remainder, putting everything she learnt together still requires practice.
- She started with outside loop (2..20) first, which caused confusion when issues came up

After going through manual steps and further clarification, she managed to get it right.

```
array = []
(2..20).each do |num|
    # check one number is a prime number or not
    flag = true
    (2..num - 1).each do |x| # try to check each possible divisor
        if num % x == 0
            flag = false # mark this has divisor
            break # no point to check more - composite, moves on to next
        end
    end
    if flag == true  # the number has no divisors
        array << num # add to prime number list
    end
end
puts "Prime numbers (up to 20) are : #{array.join(', ')}"
```

I asked her to add some comments as well.

Divide and Conquer

When writing code with looping, beginner programmers often start with outside loops. Take this exercise for example. Courtney first wrote:

```
(2..20).each do |num|
    #...
  end
```

This is not optimal. The key to this problem is to determine whether a number is a prime number or not. The outside loop checking `2..20` is just an icing on the cake. The correct order for programming this problem is

- writing code to check whether the number (variable, e.g. `num = 5`) is a prime number
- looping within the given range
- add prime numbers to a list (initialize outside the loop, add a prime number inside the loop)
- print out the list

By working on the core problem, you will have a better focus. Once you sort out the core, it is very easy to add the outside loop.

On the other hand, the outside loop and other non-core code might complicate the issue during programming, especially to inexperienced programmers. That's what happened to Courtney. Again, it takes time and practice. Keep coding and thinking to improve, you will get better on this.

6.5 Fibonacci sequence

 Start with a pair of rabbits (one male and one female) born on January 1. Assume that all months are of equal length and that :

1. the first pair of rabbits reproduced two months after their own birth;
2. after reaching the age of two months, each pair produces a mixed pair, (one male, one female), and then another mixed pair each month thereafter; and
3. no rabbit dies.

How many pairs will there be in the end of each month of first year?

```
The number of rabbit pairs are:
1, 1, 2, 3, 5, 8, 13, 21, 34, 55, 89, 144
```

Purpose

- Analyse the problem and find out its matching pattern.
- Variable assignment

Analyse

Clearly, there is a pattern on the number of rabbit pairs. To find out a pattern, we need to work out the numbers in first several months, like below.

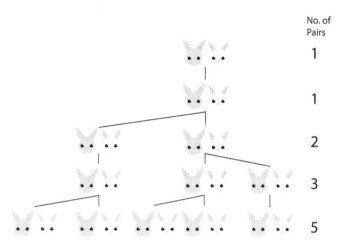

Fibonacci sequence

This is the famous 'Fibonacci sequence'. If you read the book 'Da Vinci Code', you might remember fibonacci sequence was used as the password for a safe.

Each new number in Fibonacci sequence is generated by adding the previous two numbers. By starting with 1 and 1, the first 10 numbers will be:
1, 1, 2, 3, 5, 8, 12, 21, 34, 55

Hints

Fibonacci sequence starts with first 2 numbers.

```
num1 = 1
num2 = 1
```

The algorithm behind this program might seem simple: just produce *a number that is the sum of the previous two*. This will test your understanding of variable assignments. In programming, $x = 1$ is not 'x equals to 1', instead means 'assign 1 to x'. That's why we can do number increment using $a = a + 1$, which does not make sense in Math.

```
a = 10
a = a + 1  #  now a = 11
```

The program seems simple with only a few lines of code, however, it is not as simple as you might think. If you get stuck, think about *assigning variables to a new number.*

Also, after generating a correct Fibonacci sequence, you will need to think about stopping at the 12th number (12 months).

6.6 Consecutive Sums

 Some natural numbers can be written as a sum of consecutive natural numbers. For example, 10 = 1 + 2 + 3 + 4. Some can be written in more than one way. For example, 9 = 2 + 3 + 4 and 9 = 4 + 5. Write a program to output all possible ways for a given natural number.

```
Enter a number: 9
9 = 2 + 3 + 4
9 = 4 + 5
```

Purpose

- loop within another loop with different looping variables
- loop a number range with a variable
- print array element using a custom join character

Analyse

An adding operation involves at least 2 numbers. In other words, the maximum consecutive natural number in the question can only be (x + 1) / 2. Let's call this number y.

Then we will try to find the consecutive numbers and add them as below:

```
1 + 2
  1 + 2 + 3
    # ...
    1 + 2 + 3 + ... + y
2 + 3
  2 + 3 + 4
    # ...
    2 + 3 + 4 +  ... + y
# ...
(y-1)  +  y
```

It is important to understand that there are two loops:

- the outside loop iterates the starting number
- the inside loop decides how many consecutive numbers are used for adding.

Pseudocode

```
x   is the target number
for each number (starting_number) in 1 .. y-1
  for each number j in starting_number .. y
    calculate the sum (starting_number + 1) + (starting_number + 2) + ... + j
    if the sum is equal to x
      print out
    end
  end the internal loop
end loop
```

Hints

We have done looping with a range before. For convenience, here is another example:

```
x = 10
(1..x-1).each do |i|
  print "#{i}, "
end
# will print 1, 2, 3, 4, 5, 6, 7, 8, 9,
```

To sum a range, we can convert a range into an array by using to_a first, then use the standard array summing.

```
(1..100).to_a.inject(0){|sum,item| sum + item} # => 5050
```

We have used array.join(',') to output an array in a string. In fact, you can use other join characters, such as " + " below.

```
[1, 2, 3, 4].join(" + ") # => "1 + 2 + 3 + 4"
```

6.7 Exercises

Compute PI

Write a program to compute the value of Π based on the formula.

$$\pi = 4 \times \left(1 - \frac{1}{3} + \frac{1}{5} - \frac{1}{7} + \frac{1}{9} - \frac{1}{11} + \frac{1}{13} - \frac{1}{15} + \cdots\right)$$

Compute with different iteration count: 1, 100, 10000 and 1000000. Compare your result with Ruby's built-in constant `Math::PI`. Your program shall look like:

```
Enter iteration count: 1
My computation PI = 4.0
   Ruby's PI value: 3.141592653589793
```

7. Methods

With the solution in exercise 6.2 (finding the Highest Common Factor), we can see two code fragments (getting divisors for a number) that are almost identical, which is not optimal.

```
puts "Enter first number: "
num1 = gets.chomp.to_i
puts "Enter second number: "
num2 = gets.chomp.to_i

divisors_list_1 = []
(1..num1).each do |x|
  check = num1 % x
  if check == 0
    divisors_list_1 << x
  end
end

divisors_list_2 = []
(1..num2).each do |x|
  check = num2 % x
  if check == 0
    divisors_list_2 << x
  end
end
```

In programming, the methods (also known as functions) removes duplication to make the code more readable, and most importantly, easy to maintain. A simple way of thinking the use of a method: a group of code statements that performs a task and can be reused.

A method consists of

1. **method name**. *What does it do?*
2. **parameters** (optional). *Input(s) passed to the method, the value of parameters are set by the callers, i.e. they change.*
3. **returned result**. *The result returned to the caller.*

Let's see an example method:

```
def add(a, b)
  c =  a + b
  return c
end
```

Where add is the method name, a and b are the two parameters and c is the result returned to the caller. In Ruby, return ends the method.

Method names in Ruby are in lowercase. For long method names that have more than one word, the convention is to join them with an underscore character, such as register_user. It is a good idea to name your method meaningfully that reveals its purpose.

Here are two code statements calling the add method.

```
add(1, 5)        # => 6
add(100, 500)    # => 600
```

The above looks like math functions such as $f(x) = x^2 - x + 1$. Yes, that's why methods are also called functions. For example, writing this function in Ruby will look like below:

```
def f(x)
  return x ^ 2  - x + 1
end
```

7.1 Finding the Highest Common Factor (using method)

Write a program to ask the user to enter two non-negative integers and then find the highest common factor (HCF). The program must define a method that return the divisors of a number.

```
Enter the first number: (8)
Enter the second number: (12)
The HCF of 8 and 12 is: 4
```

Purpose

- Identify duplicated code
- Remove duplication by introducing methods.

Hints

You may start with the existing solution of Exercise 6-4.

To define a method, ask the following 4 questions:

1. What does it do? (this helps to name it)
2. What shall I pass to the method?
3. What I expect to return from this method?
4. How do I use the method?

```
def get_divisors(num)
  # ...
end

divisors_list_1 = get_divisors(num_1)
divisors_list_2 = get_divisors(num_2)

# ...
```

Courtney says:

This time I still spent a long time on it because I had trouble doing the last part again and finding out the problem (I had put an array inside another array). I managed to find the problem by printing out the array and using .inspect. The method was easier than the previous one. Although I had to think about what to return.

Refactoring

The new code works the same way as our previous version, but it is better, right? The formal term to describe what you have just done in software programming is '**Code Refactoring**'. Code refactoring is the process of restructuring existing code – without changing its external behavior. To put in my simple words: "work the same outside, improved inside".

7.2 Generate Lotto Numbers (using a method)

f()

Write a program to generate 6 Lotto numbers. Lotto numbers are between 1 and 49. This time, define a method that returns a valid lotto number.

```
Your winning lotto numbers are [23, 34, 12, 6, 7, 49], good luck!
```

Purpose

- move logic into methods to simplify the code
- refer variables outside the method scope

Analyse

This time, we use a method to simplify our code logic. Our target is to get 6 random numbers from 1 to 49. If we have a method that returns a random and not-appeared-before number, the solution is simple: calling the method 6 times.

Hints

```
lotto_numbers = []

def get_next_valid_lotto_number(existing_lotto_numbers)
  # randomly generate a number
  # check existing_lotto_numbers whether it appeared before
  # return one that satisfy, otherwise try again
end

new_valid_number = get_next_valid_lotto_number
lotto_numbers << new_valid_number
```

7.3 Finding the LCM for multiple numbers (using method)

Write a program to get the lowest number that is dividable by 1, 2, 3, 4, ..., 14 and 15.

```
The lowest number that is dividable by 1 to 15 is: 360360
```

Purpose

- Use the output of a method as a parameter to call the method again

Analyse

This is to calculate the LCM for multiple numbers. We have written a program to calculate the LCM for two numbers. If we divide 15 numbers into 15 calculations of LCM for two numbers, we get the answer.

```
1,    2 => LCM
LCM,  3 => LCM
LCM,  4 => LCM
...
LCM, 15 => LCM
```

Hints

You may start with the existing solution of Ex6-3, and refactor the code into a method

```
def lcm(a, b)
  # ...
end

lcm(6, 8) # => 24
```

Then construct a loop to call this method based on our analysis.

8. File and Network

In previous exercises, we have collected data from user's input and printed output to the screen. In this chapter, we will write some programs to

- read from and write to files
- read data from Internet resources
- send emails

8.1 Calculate average score

Write a program that reads the contents of a text file containing scores of a class (0-100, one each line) and calculates the average score.

The content of the text file looks like the following:

```
84
78
...
87
```

The calculated average score is rounded to one decimal point.

```
> ruby calc_average.rb
The average score is 79.8
```

Purpose

- Read text file into a string
- Read text file line by line
- Sum a list of integers

Analyse

The student scores are stored in a text file (the file content is in a text format, i.e. recognizable when opened in text editors. Image files such as JPEG are called binary files).

- read scores and process them
- sum and calculate the average

Hints

To work with a file, we must identify its path. For example, `c:\Users\you\rubycode\score.txt` on Windows; '/Users/john/work/rubycode/score.txt' on Mac or Linux. A file path is referred as a string.

The file separator for Windows '\' is a special character when specified in a string. When used in a file path, replace the single backslash with a double backslash to escape the speical character.

```
wrong_file_path = "C:\Users\you\rubycode\data\score.txt"
puts wrong_file_path # "C:Usersyou\rubycodedata core.txt"
file_path = "C:\\Users\\you\\rubycode\\data\\score.txt"
puts file_path        # "C:\Users\you\rubycode\data\score.txt"
```

The above file paths are called absolute paths. If a file is referenced this way and the program is running on another machine, it will fail as the referenced file does not exist. The safest way is to use relative paths, i.e. the file path is relative to your program.

```
# please note double underscores before and after FILE
file_path = File.join(File.dirname(__FILE__), "files", "score.txt")
```

To read all the content of a text file into a string.

```
file_content = File.read(file_path)
puts file_content # will print out full content
```

Process the file contents line by line.

```ruby
file_content = File.read(file_path)
file_content.split.each do |line|
  # ...
end
```

8.2 Count words and lines in a text file

WC	LC
21	3

Write a program that reads the contents of a file and counts the number of words and lines in that file.

```
ruby count_words_and_lines.rb file.txt
file.txt contains 126 words in 13 lines
```

Purpose

- read command line arguments

Analyse

The program is a generic utility, which means we can use the program for different text files. Therefore, we cannot hardcode the input file path. When running a program, we can pass arguments to the program. These arguments are called command line arguments.

Hints

Read the first command line argument: ARGV[0]

```
first_command_line_argument = ARGV[0]
puts "The first argument is: #{first_command_line_argument}"
```

The following batch command to run the above program

```
ruby my_program.rb special.txt
```

will get output

```
The first argument is: special.txt
```

The file path passed to the program can either be an absolute path or a relative path to the current directory. If it is the latter, the following code can convert it to the absolute path.

```
# '.' means current directory
input_file_path =  File.join(".", first_command_line_argument)
input_file_full_path = File.expand_path(input_file_path)
```

For counting words (refer to chapter 5) and lines, you can use String's split method.

8.3 Mail merge birthday invitation cards

 Jessica is planning to invite her friends to her 12th birthday party. Instead of writing individual invitations, she wants to print them out in cards. Instead of creating documents one by one, she wants to generate a letter document (a text file) using the template below:

```
Dear {{first_name}},

I am celebrating my 12th Birthday on the 1st of April!
Come celebrate with me!

Where: 42 Greed-Island Street, Yorkshin City
When: 2PM to 5PM
RSVP: 24th March (0400-000-000 or rsvpjessica@gmail.com)

Hope to see you there,

Jessica.
```

Her friends: Pokkle, Angela, Tonpa, Toby, Biscuit, Mito, Kate, Renee, Chloe, Kelly and Melody.

Write a program to help Jessica generate multiple invitation cards as text files such as *pokkle_invitation.txt* and *angela_invitation.txt*.

Purpose

- Substitute text in a string
- Read text from text files
- Write content to text files

Analyse

This is a typical mail-merge type scenario: generating a set of documents. Each document has the same kind of information, some of the content is unique. We can create a template where parts of the document that can be substituted.

To perform a substitution, we need

- the section to be replaced in the template. For example, {{first_name}} is the one for this exercise.
- the text to replace into the template, i.e. friends' first names.

Once the text is substituted, it can be written into a text file.

Hints

Text Substitution

```
str_1 = "We scare because we care"
str_2 = str_1.gsub("scare", "laugh")  # => "We laugh because we care"
str_3 = str_1.gsub("care", "cure") # => "We scure because we cure"
```

gsub replaces certain texts in a string and returns a modified string. It does not change the original string. To make the changes, use gsub!.

```
puts str_1;  # => "We scare because we care"
str_1.gsub!("we", "he")
puts str_1;  # => "We scare because he care"
```

Write string to a text file

```
new_file_content = "Laugh is the best medicine"
File.open("c:/work/rubycode/output_1.txt", "w").write(new_file_content)
```

The first argument c:/work/rubycode/output_1.txt is the file path, the second argument 'w' indicates openning the given file for writing. To append to an existing file, use 'a' for the second argument.

8.4 Rename files

 Write a program to rename the following files in a directory so that the files are always shown in alphabetical order and without spaces.

```
chapter 1.txt      chapter_01.txt
chapter 10.txt     chapter_02.txt
chapter 11.txt     chapter_03.txt
chapter 2.txt      chapter_04.txt
chapter 3.txt      chapter_05.txt
chapter 4.txt      chapter_06.txt
chapter 5.txt      chapter_07.txt
chapter 6.txt      chapter_08.txt
chapter 7.txt      chapter_09.txt
chapter 8.txt      chapter_10.txt
From chapter 9.txt  to chapter_11.txt
```

(the directory with the above sample files can be found at *sources/files/book_dir*).

Purpose

- Process files in a directory
- Pattern matching using Regular Expression
- Rename files

Analyse

The objective is quite clear and can be divided in the following steps:

1. Iterate each file in a specified directory (by path)
2. Extract the number from the original file name, e.g. '9' from 'chapter 9.txt'
3. Construct a new file name, e.g. 'chapter_09.txt'
4. Rename the file

As you have mastered looping, it is a good idea to start with just renaming a single file. Once you have completed that, then process all the files in the directory.

Hints

Get files in a directory

```
a_directory = "c:/books"
Dir.foreach(directory) do |item|
  next if item == '.' or item == '..' # skip this and parent directory
  # do something to item
end
```

The '.' and '..' have special meanings when used in a file path: current directory and parent directory respectively. For example, the three commands below

```
> cd c:\foo\bar\ruby
> cd ..
> ..\run.exe
```

are equal to c:\foo\run.exe.

Rename files

FileUtils[1] defines a set of utility methods to manage files such as creating a new directory, copying and renaming files. FileUtils.mv(src, dest) method moves one file (by path), *renaming* is one form of 'moving'.

```
require 'fileutils' # need to require it first
FileUtils.mv("c:/books/a.txt", "c:/books/b.txt")
```

Extract text using Regular Expression

Regular Expression (abbreviated *regex* or *regexp*) is a pattern of characters that finds matching text. Nearly every programming language supports regular expression, with minor differences. Here is a typical regular expression usage in Ruby:

```
if a_str =~ /regular expression here/
  # processing matched pattern
end
```

Regular expression is very powerful and it does take some time to master it well. To get it going for simple text matching, however, is not hard. Google 'ruby regular expression' shall return some good tutorials, and Rubular[2] is a helpful tool to let you try out regular expression online.

Here is an example regression expression for this program:

---

[1]http://www.ruby-doc.org/stdlib-2.0/libdoc/fileutils/rdoc/FileUtils.html
[2]http://rubular.com/

```
my_str = "chapter 12.txt"
if my_str =~ /chapter\s(\d+)(.*)/
  $1 # => '12'
  $2 # => ".txt"
end
```

where

- \d means to match a digit, 0 - 9
- \d+ matches 1 or more digits
- \s matches a white space character
- . matches any one character
- * matches none or many any character
- () will pass matched text to special variables: $1 for first matched text, $2 for the second.

Adding leading zeros to a string

Ruby's String class has a built-in function rjust (right-justified), which makes a string to a given length with a given padding character.

```
"1".rjust(4, "0") # => '0001'

some_int = 7 # to use
some_int.to_s.rjust(3, '0')  # => '007'
some_int.to_s.rjust(5, '0')  # => '00005'
```

8.5 Currency exchange with live quoting

$\$ \leftrightarrow ¥$ Write a currency conversion program that converts Australian Dollars to Japanese Yen. To ensure we have a more accurate exchange rate, we will use Yahoo Finance's live currency rate service.

NOTE: Internet connection is required for this exercise.

```
Enter the amount of Australian dollars: 598
=> ¥ 56986.35
```

If you are unable to connect to Yahoo Finance (e.g. no internet connection), the program shall exit gracefully with an error message.

```
Unable to connect to Yahoo Finance, Error: 'getaddrinfo: nodename nor servname provided, \
or not known'
```

Purpose

- **Get content from a URL**

  Your program gets dynamic data from a URL and process it (you might have heard of a fancy name for this: Web Programming).

- **Parse JSON string**

  JSON stands for "JavaScript Object Notation", a very popular data format for exchanging data between software programs. Here is an example JSON.

  ```
  {"AUD_JPY":{"val":81.163776}}
  ```

- **Parse CSV**

  CSV ("Comma Separated Values") file format is often used to exchange data in tabular form. Below is a sample CSV file:

```
DESCRIPTION,LOGIN,PASSWORD,EXPECTED_TEXT
Valid Login,agileway,test,Login Successful!
User name not exists,nonexists,smartass,Login is not valid
```

The easiest way to view CSV files is to open in Excel.

- **Understanding API** (Application Programming Interface)

  You can think API is the way for a software program to interact with another. The API for this currency change service is to provide live exchange rates (in JSON or CSV) via HTTP protocol.

- **Error handling**

Analyse

As the requirement for this program is 'live exchange rate', we cannot use the hard-coded exchanges rates. In other words, the program shall use the current rate directly from the currency exchange market. You can see an example of live exchange rate between Australian dollar and Japanese Yen[3].

You may use one of the free exchange rate API below:

- Currency Converter API

  https://free.currencyconverterapi.com/api/v5/convert?q=AUD_JPY&compact=y

- Yahoo Finance API

  http://download.finance.yahoo.com/d/quotes.csv?s=AUDJPY=X&f=sl1d1t1ba&e=.csv

You can try it out by pasting the URL into your browser, you will see what you get back. Currency Converter API returns in JSON format; Yahoo Finance API returns CSV format.

Update: Yahoo Finance API is no longer accessible.

Hints

Get content from a URL

The Swift code below retrieves the exchange rate from a web address (called Uniform Resource Locator, URL in short).

---

[3]https://au.finance.yahoo.com/q?s=AUDJPY=X

```
require 'net/http'
require 'uri'
url_content =  Net::HTTP.get(URI.parse(url))
```

Exception handling

The above code only works if you are connected to Internet and Yahoo Finance server is up running. If not, you will get an error message like below:

```
net/http.rb:879:in `initialize': getaddrinfo: nodename nor servname provided, or not know\
n (SocketError)
```

This brings an important concept in programming: Exception handling. An exception means an anomalous or exceptional condition occurred. The code to handle exceptions is called exception handling. If an exception is not handled, the program execution will terminate with the exception displayed. Here is the exception handling syntax in Ruby:

```
begin
  # ...
rescue => e
  # code to handle the exception, usually print detail first
end
```

Let's look at an example.

```
# ...
begin
  5 / 0
rescue => e
  puts "Error occurred: #{e}!"
end

puts "I can continue."
```

During the execution, an exception is raised and then handled. Here is the output:

```
Error occurred: divided by 0!
I can continue.
```

Parse JSON

Use 'JSON' gem.

```
require 'json'
json_str = '{"AUD_JPY":{"val":81.163776}}'
json_obj = JSON.parse(json_str)
return json_obj["AUD_JPY"]["val"].to_f
```

Read CSV

```
require 'csv'
csv = CSV.parse(csv_data)   # a string
csv_first_row =  csv.shift # shift returns first row
exchange_rate = csv_first_row[1].to_f # => 95.324
```

The above code reads and parses CSV data from a string directly. To read from a file:

```
require 'csv'
customers = CSV.read('customers.csv')
```

Handling CSV files (reading from and writing to) is very useful. For more information, check out this tutorial[4].

---

[4]http://www.sitepoint.com/guide-ruby-csv-library-part/

8.6 Send individual thank you emails

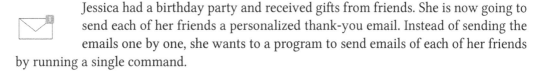 Jessica had a birthday party and received gifts from friends. She is now going to send each of her friends a personalized thank-you email. Instead of sending the emails one by one, she wants to a program to send emails of each of her friends by running a single command.

Her thank-you email looks like this:

```
Dear Angela,

Thank you for coming to my 12th birthday party, I really like the gift you gave me: Cat S\
tatue, thank you very much!

Jessica.
```

And this is a list of people (with email) and gifts she received.

- Pokkle (pokkle@archer.com): Bow and Arrows
- Angela (catlover@gmail.com): Cat Statue
- Tonpa (tonpa@hotmail.com): Juice Machine
- Toby (tobytoby123@bigpond.com): Necklace
- Biscuit (biskykruger@jewel.com): Blue Jewel
- Mito (auntiemito@gmail.com): Cooking Book
- Kate (katiecat@outlook.com): Whale Poster
- Renee (renee@travel.com): Camera
- Chloe (chloe@hunter.com): Pencil Case
- Kelly (kellyisarabbit1@bigpond.com): Rabbit Ears
- Melody (melody.456@nostrade.com): CD

How will Jessica do it?

Purpose

- Create own template file for substitution
- More complex data structure
- Use external Ruby library (gem)
- Send emails
- A chain of string substitution

Analyse

This exercise requires the use of more complex data structure and several new concepts.

By examining the sample email, we see three differences among the emails to be sent:

- Recipient's email address (in the email header)
- Recipient's first name
- The gift brought by the recipient

Therefore, we need to design a data structure to pass all the above data (for each person) to the template to generate one email. Think about the data structures you have used in Chapter 4: Array and Hash. We need to substitute more than one attribute (*first_name* and *gift*) in the template.

To send an email is quite easy. This kind of generic function is either included in Ruby or in a third party library (called RubyGems in Ruby). A modern software application uses many third party libraries, this way, no need to reinvent the wheel. The site Ruby Toolbox[5] categorizes popular ruby gems including rating and other information. The good news is that most of Ruby gems are free or charge.

---

[5]"https://www.ruby-toolbox.com/"

Avoid sending test emails to real accounts during testing

During coding, we often need to have multiple tries before get it right. Using real email addresses during coding this program is not appropriate, obviously. In other words, we would like to test email sending to different recipients but won't reach the recipients' email boxes.

Gmail has a feature to send emails to many unique email addresses while still arrive into one account, by appending '+' sign after the username:

- courtney+angela@gmail.com
- courtney+kelly@gmail.com

The emails sent to the above two addresses will arrive into *courtney@gmail.com*, and the "To:" address will keep the "+extra" you provided.

Hints

Hash in Array

We have learnt about Array (a data structure that stores a list of values), such as

```
["QLD", "NSW", "WA"]
```

and Hash, such as

```
{ "QLD" => "Brisbane", "NSW" => "Sydney", "WA" => "Perth"}
```

But what about grouping a set of related data with the same keys. It is easier to explain with an example. Let's say, I want a data structure to store the capital city and the state flower of Australian states. This data structure is different from the above, because the capital city and the state flower are different kind of data, but they both are associated to the same key: state name. How do we do that?

The answer is simple: group the capital city and the state flower. In Ruby, you can put a list of Hash in an array.

```
au_states_info = [
 {:state => "QLD", :capital => "Brisbane", :state_flower => "Cooktown Orchid"},
 {:state => "NSW", :capital => "Sydney", :state_flower => "Waratah"},
 # ...
]
```

To iterate au_states_info

```
au_states_info.each do |entry|
  entry[:state]     # first loop will be "QLD", next will be "NSW"
  entry[:capital]  # first "Brisbane", then "Sydney"
  entry[:state_flower]  # first "Cooktown Orchid"
end
```

Multiple text substitution

The following 3 statements change the string '*We scare because we care*' to '*We smile because we like*'.

```
str_1 = "We scare because we care"
str_2 = str_1.gsub("scare", "smile")
str_3 = str_2.gsub("care", "like")  # => "We smile because we like"
```

This works, however, it seems verbose. The one command achieves the same.

```
str = "We scare because we care".gsub("scare", "smile").gsub("care", "like")
```

The important concept here is that the output of the first operation `"We scare because we care".gsub("scare", "smile")` is then applied by another `gsub("care", "like")` method. This syntax is used often in coding.

Install ruby gems

Ruby gems are centrally hosted at rubygems.org[6]. To install or update a ruby gem, you need to be connected to Internet.

```
> gem install mail
```

The above command (run from a command line window) will download and install latest **mail** gem[7]. The command below lists all the gems installed on your machine.

```
> gem list
```

Configure email delivery setting

Just like using an email client (Outlook on Windows or Mail on Mac OS X) for the first time, we need to configure the setting. This is to tell the email client to use which server, user name and password. SMTP (Simple Mail Transfer Protocol) is a common protocol for email delivery. The code below configures the **Mail** gem to use Gmail.

```
# Gmail options

require 'mail'

options = {
   :enable_starttls_auto => true,
   :address => 'smtp.gmail.com',
   :port => 587,
   :authentication => 'plain',
   :user_name => 'myusername@gmail.com',  # replace with yours
   :password => 'secret'
}

Mail.defaults do
   delivery_method :smtp, options
end
```

---

[6]"http://rubygems.org"
[7]https://github.com/mikel/mail

This setting only need to be done once in the program.

Send an email

```
Mail.deliver do
  from      'me@foo.com'
  to        'you@bar.net'
  subject   'Here is the stuff I mentioned'
  body      'Body content goes here'  # or File.read('/file/path/to/body.txt')
  # optional attachments
  # add_file '/full/path/to/somefile.png'
end
```

Use a control flag

The above settings can be used to send out emails to mock email addresses. However, what happens if you want to switch to using a real email address? A more efficient way to handle this scenario is the use a 'flag'. A flag helps determine is something is true or false; this is commonly achieved by setting a boolean variable:

```
test_mode = true
# ...

if test_mode
  # ...
else
  # ...
end
```

Ternary conditional: compact if statement

We used if and else a lot, which usually requires 5 statements (by lines). Sometimes we would like a more compact form. For example, the code below sets email address based on the test_mode flag:

```ruby
if test_mode
  the_email = "mine+real@gmail.com"
else
  the_email = "real@outlook.com"
end

Mail.deliver do
  to  the_email
  # ...
end
```

The code works, but it seems verbose. Ruby's ternary operator(also called ternary conditional) is a shorthand for `if ... else`. The general format of this expression is as follows:

condition ? true : false

The code above can be refactored (means enhanced without changing its outcome) as below using Ternary Condition:

```ruby
Mail.deliver do
  to  test_mode ? "mine+real@gmail.com" : "real@gmail.com"
  # ...
end
```

Code is for computers as well as Human

While the code is for machines to execute, don't forget its another important audience: human being. Software requires regular updates and being maintained, you and fellow programmers will need to understand and modify the code some time later. By then, well written code will make future work easier, more importantly, reduce the chance of introducing defects. This might take years to master, but I would suggest developing habits to put some thoughts for code quality when programming.

8.7 Exercises

GradesHistogram

Write a program that reads grades (between 0 and 100, integer) from a text file and display the histogram.

For example:

```
49 50 51 59 0 5 9 10 15 19 50 68 55 89 100 99
```

Output:

```
 0 -  9: ***
10 - 19: ***
20 - 29:
30 - 39:
40 - 49: *
50 - 59: *****
60 - 69: *
70 - 79:
80 - 89: *
90 -100: **
```

9. Object Oriented Programming

Ruby is an object-oriented programming language. Please bear with me if you have no idea what object-oriented is.

I remember that it took me quite a while to understand object-oriented concept when I was at university back in early 90s. I had no tools to try, just read theories from books. It turned out to be quite simple if it was illustrated with examples. Here is one:

Car is a class, a type of something, it has following two functions (plus many more...):

- accelerate
- brake

My car (the one in my garage) is an object of Car, it can do 'brake' and 'accelerate'. I can physically drive it.

Now have a think about statements below:

```ruby
my_car = Car.new
my_car.accelerate
your_camry = Car.new
your_camry.brake
```

You may recall some code we have used:

```ruby
a_string = "Ruby is cool"
a_string.size  # => 12
iphones = ["iPhone 4s", "iPhone 5S", "iPhone 5C"]
iphones.sort #=>["iPhone 4s", "iPhone 5C", "iPhone 5S"]
```

a_string is an object of class String, and iphones is an object of class Array. Here is how to find out an object's class.

```
a_string.class # => String
iphones.class # => Array
```

The reason we are able to call `.size` and `.sort` is because these methods are defined in the `String` and `Array` classes respectively.

Most modern programming languages support Object-oriented programming (OOP). Mastering OOP is a must for programmers nowadays.

9.1 Calculator (Class)

 Write a Calculator class that contains two methods:

- Add two numbers
- Subtract two numbers

```
puts calc.add(2, 3)  # => 5
puts calc.minus(17, calc.add(2, 3) ) # => 12
```

Purpose

- Define a class
- Define methods in a class
- Create a new instance (object) of a class
- Invoke a method on an object

Analyse

This program is quite easy if using standard methods (Chapter 7). The purpose of this exercise is to do it in a class, object-oriented way. If you understand the basic Ruby Class syntax and usage (see below), this exercise is quite straightforward.

Hints

define a class

A Ruby Class name needs to in capital case, for example, "BankAccount".

```
class BankAccount

  # ...

end
```

define methods in a class

The definition of methods in classes are the same as standard methods (Chapter 7), except that they are within the scope of a class. To put simply, the methods in a class are only available to its objects.

```
class BankAccount

  def transfer(amount, another_account)
    # ...
  end

end
```

create objects using *new* method

Objects are instances of the class.

```
require 'bank_account.rb' # if BankAccount is defined in another file
saving_account = BankAccount.new
cheque_account = BankAccount.new
```

invoke an object's method

```
saving_account.transfer(100, cheque_account)
```

9.2 Age of Teacher and Students

 A school consists of teachers and students, and students are grouped by grades. Write a program to calculate

- a teacher's age
- the average age of teachers
- the average age of Grade 10 students

```
teacher_1 = Teacher.new("James Bond", "1968-04-03")  # name, birthday
teacher_2 = Teacher.new("Michael Zasky", "1978-01-02")

students = []
students << Student.new("John Sully", "1999-10-03", 10)  # 10 is grade
students << Student.new("Michael Page", "1999-05-07", 11)
students << Student.new("Anna Boyle", "1998-12-03", 10)
students << Student.new("Dominic Chan", "1999-09-10", 10)
```

Output:

```
Teacher 'James Bond' age: 46
Average Teacher age: 41.0
The number of Grade 10 students: 3
Average Grade 10 students age: 15.0
```

Purpose

- Instance variables
- Read and write instance variables
- Class Constructor
- Class Inheritance
- Age calculation
- Use of array operations (review)

Analyse

The core function is to calculate ages, and we have two identified Classes Teacher and Student (from the code fragment). We could write two get_age functions in both Teacher and Student classes, however this is not correct. You wouldn't want to write another get_-age method to support another class AdminStaff.

Calculating ages (from birth date) is a common function for human. In OOP, we can move common methods into its parent class, then its child classes inherit them. This is called "Inheritance" (see hints below). For this exercise, we can create another class Person with age method, then make Teacher and Student inherit from Person. Here is the class diagram for the design.

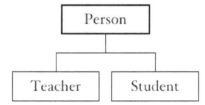

After deciding the class design at high level, we turn to Class internals. Each teacher or student has name and birthdate (needed for calculating the age). Student also shall have a grade. These are attributes of a Class, also known as "class instance variables" (see hints below).

Let me illustrate with an example:

```
John Sully is a 10 Grade student, he was born in 1999-10-23
James Bond is a teacher, born in 1968-10-03
```

The information can be represented in this code:

```
john_sully = Student.new("John Sully", "1999-10-23", 10)
james_bond = Teacher.new("James Bond", "1968-04-03")
```

where john_sully is an object (or instance) of class Student and james_bond is an object of class Teacher. The data in brackets were stored in each object's attributes.

```
john_sully.grade # => 10
james_bond.name  # => "James Bond"
```

The business function of this exercise is to calculate age from birth date. We all know how to do it: comparing the birth date against today's date. However, this can be a bit tricky. See hints for how to use Ruby's built-in date helper methods.

Hints

Class instance variables

A class usually has certain attributes, such as "Person has name, birth date, ...".

```
class Person
  def name
    return @name # instance variable
  end
end

person = Person.new
person.name # = nil
person.name = "Courtney" # => no method error
```

We can read the name, but couldn't assign the name. So we add a writer method.

```
class Person
  def name
    @name
  end

  def name=(str)
    @name = str
  end
end

person = Person.new
person.name = 'Dominic'
person.name # => "Dominic"
```

Now we can read and write instance variable @name using reader and writer methods. As this is used very often, Ruby has a simple way:

```
class Person
  attr_reader :name
  attr_writer :name
end
```

and even simpler:

```
class Person
  attr_accessor :name
end
```

Class Constructor

Assuming we have a class `Person` with two attributes `name` and `birth_date` (defined as above using `attr_accessor`), the code below creates two `Person` objects.

```
john_smith = Person.new
john_smith.name = "John Smith"
john_smith.birth_date = "2000-01-01"

mary_boyle = Person.new
mary_boyle.name = "Mary Boyle"
mary_boyle.birth_date = "1999-10-21"
```

Calling `Class.new` creates an object of the class. There is a special method inside Class to respond to this operation: `initialize`. This method is also called "Constructor". Except its special meaning (returning a new object) and predefined method name `initialize`, the syntax of a constructor is pretty much like a method.

```
class Person
  attr_accessor :name, :birth_date

  # constructor
  def initialize(a_name, a_birth_date)
    @name = a_name
    @birth_date = a_birth_date
  end

end
```

By using our own constructor, we can create person objects in a more readable form.

```
john_smith = Person.new("John Smith", "2000-01-01")
mary_boyle = Person.new("Mary Boyle", "1999-10-21")
```

Class Inheritance

Inheritance is a relation between two classes. For example, seagulls and parrots are both birds, thus they share the common features of birds.

```
class Bird
  def fly
    puts "I am flying"
  end
end

class Seagull < Bird
end

class Parrot < Bird
  def speak
    puts "if someone teaches me"
  end
end

seagull = Seagull.new
seagull.fly    # => "I am flying"

parrot = Parrot.new
parrot.fly     # => "I am flying"
parrot.speak   # => "if someone teaches me"

seagull.speak # NoMethodError: undefined method `speak' for #<Seagull:0x..>
```

By using inheritance, the code (defined in methods) can be reused.

Override methods

Child classes may override its parent behavior by supplying new implementation: defining the same method with different statements inside.

```
class Ostrich < Bird
  def fly
    puts "I'd rather run"
  end
end

ostrich = Ostrich.new
ostrich.fly #=> "I'd rather run"
```

Date calculation

Ruby has built-in date helper methods.

```
require 'date' # need to load first, assume today is 2014-11-25
Date.today.to_s  # => "2014-11-07"
Date.today.class  # => Date
Date.today.year  = 2014
Date.today.month = 11
Date.today.day   = 25
```

The above date methods such as `.month` are defined in Date class. Commonly, we start with a date string (user entered), to convert a `Date` object:

```
Date.parse("2014-01-29") # => a date object
```

For more Date methods, see doc[1].

_____

[1]http://www.ruby-doc.org/stdlib-2.1.1/libdoc/date/rdoc/Date.html

9.3 Calculate Sales Tax

!0%
GST

The sales tax in Australia is called Goods and services tax (GST) of 10%, which is applied to most products and services. For example, in a physio clinic, medical services such as physiotherapy is GST-free, however GST applies to pilates classes (also a service), so is to all products sold at the clinic. All business must show "GST-inclusive prices". For example, for a $10 meal, $9.09 is net amount and $0.91 is sales tax.

Complete the program below to calculate the net amount and sales tax of product and services.

```
# ... define Class Goods and ServiceItem

foam_roller = Goods.new("Foam Roller", 49.95)
physio_service = ServiceItem.new("Physio Consultation", 120.0)
pilates_class = ServiceItem.new("Pilates Classes", 80.0)
pilates_class.sales_tax_applicable = true
# ... statements to print out product and services' net amount and sale tax
```

Output:

```
Foam Roller Net Amount: 45.41, GST: 4.54
Physio Consultation Net Amount: 120.0, GST: 0.0
Pilates Classes Net Amount: 72.73, GST: 7.27
```

Purpose

- Class Design
- Module and Mixin
- Class Constructor setting default value of instance variables

Analyse

From the given code fragment, two classes Goods and ServiceItem need to be defined. The sales tax calculation code is shared between the two classes. There are two common approaches to achieve code reuse:

- Inheritance
- Mixin

We have used 'Inheritance' in the previous exercise. Here we will be using 'Mixin'. Before we get to 'Mixin', we need to understand a new concept `Module`. A `Module` is another way to group a set of methods and constants. Below is an example:

```
module A

  def a
  end

  def b
  end

end
```

As you can see, it is quite similar to `Class` in terms of syntax and structure. You may wonder, why bother `module`? When a module is included in a class (Mixin), its methods are available to the class instances, i.e., code reuse. The difference of class inheritance: Mixin is about providing methods that you can use across multiple classes; Inheritance is more about structure (attributes and methods).

Effective use of Mixin can make your Ruby code more flexible and concise. Popular Ruby on Rails framework uses Mixins extensively.

For this exercise, as GST calculation is the same, it makes sense to create a module `GSTCalc` containing GST-calcluation methods.

```
module GSTCalc
  GST_RATE = 10.0

  def net_amount
    # ...
  end

  def gst
    # ...
  end

end
```

Then you can include the module in your classes: Mixin.

```
class ServiceItem
  include GSTCalc
  # ...
end

class Goods
  include GSTCalc
  # ...
end

foam_roller = Goods.new("Foam Roller", 49.95)
foam_roller.gst  # calling the method in GSTCalc
```

Hints

 The concept of Mixin can be quite confusing to beginners, certainly was the case for Courtney. I would recommend writing the program in the standard OO way:

- Design the Classes first
- Identify their attributes
- Identify their methods
- Implement the methods

Then try to introduce Mixin to optimize the program: remove the code duplication.

Setting default value to instance variables in the constructor

Quite common, the value of certain instance variables are the same for most cases. Instead of an parameter in the class constructor, we could set the default value. If necessary, we can change its value via a setter method (object.attr =).

```
class Student
 attr_accessor :name, :is_talented

 def initialize(a_name)
   @name = a_name
   @is_talented = false
 end
end

john = Student.new("John Smith")
john.is_talented    #=> false

newton = Student.new("Newton")
newton.is_talented = true
newton.is_talented  #=> true
```

Module example: Logging

The module below provides message logging (print out in a formatted way, typically to a file).

```
module Logging

  def log(message)
    puts "[#{Time.now}] [#{self.class.name}] #{message}"
  end

end
```

To utilize the logging, we need to add `include Logging` in the class.

```
class A
  include Logging
end

class B
  include Logging
end

class C
end
```

```
a = A.new
b = B.new
c = C.new

a.log("in A") # => [2014-11-08 16:07:32 +1000] [A] in A
b.log("in B") # => [2014-11-08 16:07:32 +1000] [B] in B
c.log("in C") # => undefined method `log' for #<C:xxx> (NoMethodError)
```

`c.log()` failed because the class `C` did not include the `Logging` module, therefore the method `log` is not available. Please note that output the log message printed out class names dynamically based on which class it is called from.

Access instance variables in module methods

Once a module is loaded in a class (Mixin), its method is called as a method defined in the class. In this exercise, the `sales_tax_applicable` attribute of class `ServiceItem` obviously affects the GST calculation.

```
physio_service = ServiceItem.new("Physio Consultation", 120.0)
pilates_class = ServiceItem.new("Pilates Classes", 80.0)
pilates_class.sales_tax_applicable = true
```

This means in our `GSTCalc` module, it must refer the instance variable `@sales_tax_applicable`.

```
module GSTCalc
  # ...

  def gst
    if @sales_tax_applicable    # check the object's instance variable
      # ...
    else
      return 0.0
    end
  end

end
```

9.4 Library System

 Implement a simplified library system. Initially, the librarian can import book records into the system via a CSV file. Members of the library can borrow and return books.

```
Library.import_books(File.join(File.dirname(__FILE__), "files","books.csv"))
Library.book_count # => 10
```

The format of CSV file:

```
TITLE, AUTHOR
The 4-Hour Workweek, Timothy Ferriss
How to Win Friends and Influence People, Dale Carnegie
```

Here is an example use of the library system:

```
john = Member.new("John Sully", "1001")
mike = Member.new("Mike Zasky", "1002")

book = Library.find_by_title("Practical Web Test Automation")
Library.borrow(john, book)
# Output "OK"
Library.borrow(mike, book)
# Output: The book 'Practical Web Test Automation' is not available!
Library.return(book)
Library.borrow(mike, book)
# Output "OK"
```

Purpose

- Class Methods
- Class Variables
- Class Design
- Load CSV data into objects
- Find matching objects in an array

Analyse

By examining the nouns in the description of this exercise, we can identify 3 classes:

- **Book**

  Book has two attributes: `title` and `author`.

- **Member**

  Member has two attributes: `name` and `member_id`.

- **Library**

  The main class for this exercise. Library members belong to the library, so are the books. So `Library` has to attributes: books and members. Because there will be only one instance of `Library`, we don't need to create it, just use `Library` class directly.

  books and members are class variables (see hints below) of `Library`. `borrow`, `return` and `find_by_title` are `Library`'s class methods.

Not all classes can be directly extracted from the problem description. For example, book lending is associated to records, a `Rental` class.

- **Rental**

  borrowing records containing the member and the book (not the book title as there can be multiple copies of the same book). The rental records can be used check a member's borrowing history and a book's lending history.

Hints

Class Variables and Class Methods

In comparison to instance variables, class variables are shared by all instances of a Class. Let me illustrate with an example,

- john's car is Honda Accord
- mike's car is Toyota Camry

Both cars are Sedan, I can represent this in Ruby Class:

```
class Sedan
  attr_accessor :make, :model

  def initialize(make, model)
   @make = make
   @model = model
  end
end

johns_car = new Sedan("Honda", "Accord")
mikes_car = new Sedan("Toyota", "Camry")
```

Obviously, the make and model are instance variables, as different objects may have different values. Now, if I ask you how many wheels does John's car or Mike's car have? The answer is 4. In fact, 4 is the answer to all sedans. The number_of_wheels is a Class Variable of Sedan:

```
class Sedan

  @@number_of_wheels = 4

  # definition of a class method, starting with self.
  def self.number_of_wheels
    return @@number_of_wheels
  end

end

Sedan.number_of_wheels  # => 4
```

Library's Class variables

```
class Library
  @@books = []
  @@members = []
  @@rentals = []

  # ...
end
```

Library's Class Methods

```
class Library

  def self.import_books(file)
    # read CSV and create book objects (see the hint below)
  end

  def self.borrow(member, book)
    # create rental object
    # update book status
  end

  # and more ...
end
```

A checked out book is not available to borrow, have a think about how to ensure that.

Load CSV data into objects

Parse the CSV file (we covered CSV in Chapter 8), then create objects from the data.

```
require 'csv'
CSV.foreach(csv_file) do |row|
  next if row[0] == 'TITLE' # skip the heading row
  a_book = Book.new
  a_book.title = row[0]
  a_book.author = row[1]
  a_book.status = "available"
  @@books << a_book
end
```

Find matching objects in an array

Using Array's built-in select method.

```ruby
def self.find_by_title(book_title)
  the_book = @@books.select{|x| x.title == book_title }.first
  if the_book.nil?
    puts "Book #{book_title} not found"
  end
  return the_book
end
```

9.5 Sunflower vs Zombies Game Simulation

 This is a simplified simulation of the famous "Plants vs Zombies" Game. A sunflower is on the left of the field, zombies come towards the sunflower (to eat it) one by one. The purpose of the game is to let the sunflower to survive one wave of attack (15 zombies).

Each step a zombie makes, there will be "exchange of fire" (the sunflower shoots seeds to the zombie; the zombie throws stones to the sunflower), both the sunflower and the zombie receive a certain degree of damage to their health. If the attacking zombie's health down to 0%, the zombie dies and then comes another until no more. If the sunflower's health reaches 0%, game over.

Game rules:

- The health level of the sunflower and zombies start at 100%
- Zombie needs to travel 10 steps to get to the sunflower
- During 'exchange of fire', the damage to the zombie and the sunflower are nondeterministic. The sunflower receives a lot less damage than the zombie.
- If a zombie arrives next to the sunflower, it will cause bigger damage to the sunflower.
- There is a rare specie of Jump Zombie who can move two steps at a time.
- The game speed is adjustable.

User Interface (UI) requirement:

This simulation is dynamically presented in text (not graphic), the zombies and the sunflower are represented as Z(health) and F(health) respectively. The movement of zombies is indicated by placing the zombie in the field as below.

```
F(100)   ___ ___ ___ ___ ___ ___ ___ ___ ___ Z87
F( 98)   ___ ___ ___ ___ ___ ___ ___ ___ Z38 ___
F( 95)   ___ ___ ___ ___ ___ ___ ___ Z00 ___ ___
```

While the above show 3 lines of printed out text, in the simulation, there shall be only one (see hints). The line text is re-printed again and again to achieve a "Motion" effect.

if the sunflower wins,

```
F( 11)   ___ ___ ___ ___ ___ ___ ___ Z00 ___ ___
```

You Win! Flower survived attacks from 15 zombies.

if the zombies win,

```
F(  0)   ___ ___ ___ ___ ___ ___ Z18 ___ ___ ___
```

Game Over! 2 zombies left.

Purpose

- Game Design
- Use of Class Variables and Class Methods
- Overwrite previously printed line

Analyse

This program is quite complex, as always, it is a good idea to start with class design.

Clearly, we have two classes: Sunflower and Zombie. There are one Sunflower instance and 15 Zombie instances. The health attributes of both classes are used to determine live or death of an object.

The distance a zombie has travelled can be used for determining whether to apply "close-combat damage". Jump Zombie moves 2 steps at one go, so there should be a speed attribute.

After defined the attributes, we move on to the methods (or behaviours).

Flower

- *exchange_fire*: called when a zombie move forward a step. This records the damage to the sunflower and the only zombie in the field. We can add randomness there to increase unpredictability of simulation.
- *die*: health down to 0%.

Zombie

- *move_forward*: move one or two steps based on the object's speed.

- *die*: health down to 0%.

We can also add some helper methods such as `is_dead?`, `in_touch_distance?`.

With the class design completed, we move to the game engine. The game is running as long as the sunflower is alive and there are zombies remaining. A typical `while` loop here. Within each loop,

- check and locate the next zombie. The game ends if no more.
- the active zombie move forward a step (or two steps if is a Jumpy) and exchange fire with the sunflower.
- print out the "battle scene"

Hints

CONSTANTS

A constant is like a variable, except that its value is supposed to remain constant for the duration of the program. A Ruby constant's name starts with an upper case letter, commonly all upper cases.

```
NUMBER_OF_ZOMBIES = 10
```

If you change the value of a constant later, Ruby will give a warning, though the value is still modified.

```
# ...
NUMBER_OF_ZOMBIES = 15 # warning: already initialized constant
```

Using class variables in the game

```ruby
class Zombie
  @@live_count = 0

  def initialize
    # ...
    @@live_count += 1
  end

  def self.remaining_lives
    @@live_count
  end
end
```

```ruby
zombies = []
3.times { zombies << Zombie.new }
puts Zombie.remaining_lives # => 3
```

Create Jump Zombies

```ruby
attr_accessor :moving_speed

def initialize
  # ...
  @moving_speed = rand(10) >= 8  ?  2 : 1 # 20% chances are jumping zombies
end
```

@moving_speed is used in `move_forward()` function to reflect a zombie's traveling pace.

Overwrite previously printed line

We used `puts` a lot, which prints out text and a new line. To just print out text, use `print`.

```ruby
puts "Good"
puts "Morning"
print "See "
print "You"
print "Later"
```

Output:

```
Good
Morning
See YouLater
```

To overwrite previously printed line, add \r (carriage return without a line feed).

```
print "First Line"
sleep 1  # to see "First Line" displayed briefly
#... no other puts or print statements
print "\rSecond Line"
```

The final output will be only "Second Line".

9.6 Exercises

Calculate Shape Area

Define four classes: Shape, Rectangle, Triangle and Square. Define area method and attributes in these classes to calculate the shape area. The usage like below:

```
puts Triangle.new(10, 5).area()
puts Rectangle.new(10, 5).area()
puts Square.new(10).area()
```

Try using Class Inheritance as possible.

Hints

Draw a diagram like the one in Exercise 9.2 first.

10. Classic Puzzles

In this chapter, we will use our coding skills to solve some fun puzzles. You might have seen them before, but solving it with code will be more interesting.

10.1 Google Labs Aptitude Test

 Solve this cryptic equation, every letter represent a distinct number between 0 - 9. No leading zeros are allowed. (This was a Google Interview question).

```
    WWWDOT
  - GOOGLE
  --------
    DOTCOM
```

Purpose

- Using nested loops
- Trying with unique numbers within nested loops

Analyse

We have 9 letters here.

```
  W D O T G L E C M
```

W, G and D cannot be 0.

A brute-force way is to try every combination of 26 alphabetic characters using fast computing power of the computers:

- W = 1, D = 0, O = 0, T = 0, G = 0, L = 0, E = 0, C = 0, M = 0
- W = 1, D = 0, O = 0, T = 0, G = 0, L = 0, E = 0, C = 0, M = 1
- W = 1, D = 0, O = 0, T = 0, G = 0, L = 0, E = 0, C = 0, M = 2
- ...
- W = 1, D = 0, O = 0, T = 0, G = 0, L = 0, E = 0, C = 0, M = 9
- W = 1, D = 0, O = 0, T = 0, G = 0, L = 0, E = 0, C = 1, M = 0

..., until find a solution.

We all know that this is not efficient. However, sometimes a simple solution utilising computing power is not a bad idea.

For these 9 letters, each represents a unique digit (0-9). Brute force method means trying 1 - 9 for W, within this loop, trying 0-9 for 'D' until to the 9th letter M. The core logic is within the most inner loop:

- construct the top number (WWWDOT)
- construct the bottom number (GOOGLE)
- construct the result (DOTCOM)
- print out the solution if the top number minus the bottom number is equal to the result

A brute force approach usually takes quite a while to solve, due to a large number of looping. It is important to add constraints to reduce the number of loops (the code checking the calculation). For example, by adding checking for uniqueness (if W is 1, D cannot be 1, O cannot be equal to W and D, ..., etc), the number of effective loops is reduced to 2,540,160, from possible 729,000,000!

Hints

Nested Loops

The code below prints a 9x9 times table.

```
for i in 1..9 do
  for j in 1..9 do
    puts "#{i}x#{j} = #{i*j}"
  end
end
```

Output:

```
1 x 1 = 1
1 x 2 = 2
1 x 3 = 3
1 x 4 = 4
1 x 5 = 5
1 x 6 = 6
1 x 7 = 7
1 x 8 = 8
1 x 9 = 9
2 x 1 = 2
2 x 2 = 4
...
9 x 9 = 81
```

Construct a number from digits

```
a = 3
b = 6
c = 5
num_days = a * 100 + b * 10 + c  # => 365
```

10.2 Fibonacci and HCF (Recursion)

 We have done the Fibonacci exercise before. This time, we will use Recursion. Before I explain what is Recursion, let's examine the formula of Nth Fibonacci number:

```
fib(1) = 1
fib(2) = 1
fib(n) = fib(n-1) + fib(n-2)
```

If I asked "what is the 6th fibonacci number?", many can answer quickly. What if I change the question to 674th Fibonacci number? By now, I hope you have developed the habit of "thinking" like a computer. Back to the question, have a look at this worksheet.

fib(6) = fib(5) + fib(4)   fib(6) = 5 + 3 = 8

    fib(5) = fib(4) + fib(3)   fib(5) = 3 + 2 = 5

       fib(4) = fib(3) + fib(2)   fib(4) = 2 + 1 = 3

          fib(3) = fib(2) + fib(1)   fib(3) = 1 + 1 = 2

fib(2) =1, fib(1) = 1

As you see, we don't know the answer to fib(6), fib(5) and fib(4). Until we reach `fib(3)` = `fib(2)` + `fib(1)`, as `fib(2)` and `fib(1)` are known. Then we use the result to work backwards to get fib(4), fib(5) and fib(6). This is a Recursion method.

Recursion refers to a method which solves a problem by solving a smaller version of the problem and then using that result to work out the answer to the original problem. In the context of programming, **a recursive method calls itself**. This might seem complex and hard to comprehend. If we change the thinking angle, it actually can be quite natural to certain problems.

Recursion can only be a applied to certain problems; where the problem (usually in a form of a formula) can be broken into smaller problems, like Fibonacci. Here is a solution to Fibonacci:

```
def fibonacci(n)
  return n  if n <= 1
  ( fibonacci(n - 1) + fibonacci(n - 2) )
end
puts fibonacci(10) # => 55
```

The code is quite concise, isn't it? Let's examine this code.

1. **Method definition with parameters**.

   `def fibonacci(n)` is a normal method, but it is called twice within the method self. The parameters of a recursion method is important.

2. **End cause**.

   Without that, a method calling itself will lead to an infinite loop. `return n if n <= 1` means if the parameter n is less than or equal to 1, the call returns a result back. This only ends the current method call, its result will be returned to other recursive method calls that have been waiting.

3. **Calculation with calling itself**.

   The core logic is based on the identified formula.

Try using recursion to solve Highest Common Factor (HCF) problem with Euclidean algorithm[1], a much more efficient way. The algorithm:

```
hcf(a, 0) = a
hcf(a, b) = hcf(b, a mod b)
```

Hints

Math Mod

The remainder of a division.

```
10 % 4  # => 2
```

---

[1]http://en.wikipedia.org/wiki/Greatest_common_divisor#Using_Euclid.27s_algorithm

10.3 Calculate Compound Interest

 We earn interest on the money deposited in the bank. The interest we receive for the first year will be added to the principal (and then calculate the interest for the next year), this is called Compound Interest. Write a program to calculate how much money you will receive back at the given rate after certain years.

```
Enter deposited amount : $10000
Enter interest rate (8% enter 0.08): 0.06
For how long (years): 12

After 12 years, you will get $20121.96
```

Purpose

- Recursion
- Review reading user input and printing formatted output

Analyse

Calculating compound interest, maybe less obvious than Fibonacci sequence, can also be solved with recursion. The essence of the compound interest is that the principal (money we deposit in the bank) plus the interest of the year becomes the new principal for the next year.

Hints

Make effective use of parameters of a recursion method.

```
# ...
the_total = compound_interest(amount, rate, years)
```

Recursion

```
principal = principal + rate * principal # new principal for this year
compound_interest(principal, rate, years-1)
```

Rule of 72 for estimating compound interest

A quicker way to find out the number of years requires to double your money at a given interest rate: Divide the interest rate into 72. For example, if the interest rate is 8%, 72 / 8 ⇒ 9 years.

Verify Rule of 72 with your program.

10.4 Farmer Crosses River Puzzle

 A farmer wants to cross a river and take with him a wolf, a goat, and a cabbage. There is a boat that can fit himself plus either the wolf, the goat, or the cabbage. If the wolf and the goat are alone on one shore, the wolf will eat the goat. If the goat and the cabbage are alone on the shore, the goat will eat the cabbage.

How can the farmer bring the wolf, the goat, and the cabbage across the river?

```
Step 0
[] <=  [:farmer, :wolf, :sheep, :cabbage]
Step 1 [:farmer, :sheep] forward
[:farmer, :sheep] <=  [:wolf, :cabbage]
Step 2 [:farmer] backward
[:sheep] <=  [:farmer, :wolf, :cabbage]
Step 3 [:farmer, :wolf] forward
[:farmer, :wolf, :sheep] <=  [:cabbage]
Step 4 [:farmer, :sheep] backward
[:wolf] <=  [:farmer, :sheep, :cabbage]
Step 5 [:farmer, :cabbage] forward
[:farmer, :wolf, :cabbage] <=  [:sheep]
Step 6 [:farmer] backward
[:wolf, :cabbage] <=  [:farmer, :sheep]
Step 7 [:farmer, :sheep] forward
[:farmer, :wolf, :sheep, :cabbage] <=  []
Done!
```

Purpose

- Backtracking algorithm

Analyse

Remember your first attempts on this famous puzzle, maybe like this:

1. Choose farmer and over the river, oops, back.
2. Choose farmer and sheep over the river, check, good.
   1. farmer back, still good.

    2. farmer and cabbage cross, OK.

    3. farmer back, oops! back.

3. ...

This trial and error method is called backtracking in programming. Backtracking is an algorithmic paradigm that tries different possibilities until a solution is found.

```
make_a_move {

  if all crossed river? {
    print out all moves
    exit
  }

  for each four items including the farmer {

    move the item with the farmer, if item is farmer just move him

    if is_safe? and has_not_done_this_move_before? {
      make_a_move
    } else {
      undo_the_move
    }
  }
}
```

End cause

All three items and the farmer crossed the river.

Constraints

1. Farmer does not cross river empty handed as there is no point of doing that. He can come back empty handed though.
2. The item to be moved has to be on the same side with the farmer
3. Safety check
   - sheep and cabbage cannot be on the same side without the farmer
   - wolf and sheep cannot be on the same side without the farmer
4. The move has not been done before

Hints

Data Design

> "Algorithms + Data Structures = Programs" is a famous book by Niklaus Wirth, published in 1976.

For a complex program, it is important to design the data structure at first. Data structure is how the data is organized and stored in the program; Algorithm is how a program to solve a program, using the data.

Besides simple data types (such as Integer and String), we have used the following composite types:

- Array
- Hash
- Class

For this puzzle, the data structures are relatively simple.

```
@item_positions = { :farmer => :not_crossed, :wolf => :not_crossed, :sheep => :not_crosse\
d, :cabbage => :not_crossed }
@items = [:farmer, :wolf, :sheep, :cabbage]
@direction = :forward  # default, another value :backward
```

I used instance variables @xxx here. As this is a quite complex program, several methods will be used. By using instance variables, I can use them in any methods without worrying about the scopes.

Once the data is defined, it is not hard to write the following methods:

- check whether all items are crossed?

```
def is_all_crossed_river?
  # check for @item_positions
end
```

- is safe to cross?

```
def is_safe?
  # check @item_positions, both sides!
end
```

- is the item with the farmer?

```
def is_item_with_farmer?(item)
  # check @item_positions
end
```

- move one item (with or just the farmer)

```
def move(item)
  # change value for the item and the farmer in @item_positions
  # toggle @direction
end
```

- undo the previous move as it does not satisfy the constraints

```
def undo_move(item)
  # revert value for the item and the farmer in @item_positions
  # toggle @direction
end
```

Store moving log

We need to keep a record of every movement made so that we can print out the solution.

```
# moving log starts with all in one side
@moving_log = { 0 => @item_positions.dup }
```

The above statement stores the step number and the items position in a hash. dup stands for 'duplicate'; this creates a copy of the object so that the original object won't be affected by changes.

For every move, we add it to the @moving_log. When reaching the solution (all items crossed), we print out the moving log.

There is also another use of the moving log: check whether a move has already been done?

```
def has_done_before?
  # check the moving log whether have seen current item positions before?
end
```

Backtracking

This is the core part of the program: the recursive method. Its purpose: make a move if satisfies the constraints.

```
def cross

  if is_all_crossed_river?
    # print moving log
    # exit
  end

  @items.each do |item|
    # ignore if not satifsying a move, eg. not going with the farmer
    # move item

    if is_safe? && !has_done_before? # seems OK after the move
      # add the moving log
      # increment step
      cross();  # try next move, recursive
    else
      # undo the move
    end

  end
end
```

10.5 Cryptic Math Equation (Backtracking)

Solve this cryptic equation, each letter stands for a unique digit (0-9). There are no leading zeros.

```
        UK
       USA
+     USSR
   --------
     AGING
```

Purpose

- Backtracking to solve number puzzles

Analyse

The brute-force approach (we used in Google Labs Aptitude Test) will work for this puzzle, but won't be elegant. We could use backtracking to solve this puzzle.

We have 8 letters here.

```
U K S A R G I N
```

For each letter, possible values are 0 - 9. Then our backtracking algorithm can be

- Starting with first letter 'U', assign it posssible value '0'
- Then next letter 'K', assign another possible value '1' as long as it has not been used before
- Up to the last letter 'N', then we get a combination
- Check the combination, if not match (most likely), go back one step
- Assign next possible value to 'N', check the new combination
- If run out of possible values for 'N', go back one more step
- Try assign next possible value to 'I'

This might sound complex, but it is how our brain works for a similar but much more simpler puzzles (like 2 or 3 letters). Computers don't mind complex calculations and memorizing all the steps as long as there are algorithm-turned-into-instructions to follow on. Here is the pseudocode for the above backtracking algorithm:

Pseudocode

```
function find_out(letter_index)

  if all letters are assigned
    check the answer (converting letter to digits to verify the equation)
    print out solution if matches
    return  # a combination of all 8 letters has been tried
  end

  for each digit (0-9)
    if satisfy the constraints and the digit not used
      mark the digit has been used
      assign a digit to this letter (by index)
      find_out(next_letter)
      # the above recurive call returns means 8 letters have been checked
      # make the digit available for next try
      mark the digit not used
    end
end
```

As you can imagine, this will generate a huge number of combinations to check against the equation. It is going to be slow.

Based on the equation, we can reason out

- A = 1, U = 9

  Because "USSR" plus 3-digit number (and another 2-digit) can only make 1????, i.e. A = 1 and U = 9.

- G = 0

  Based on A = 1 and U = 9, G must be 0 as U(9) carry 1 to AG (10).

We could go further, but I think this is good enough. Let's leave the rest to the computer to figure out.

End cause

The combination satisfy "UK + USA + USSR = AGING"

Constraints

1. A cannot be 0 (no leading zeroes)
2. U cannot be 0
3. A = 1
4. U = 9
5. G = 0
6. The digit must has not been used to assign to a letter

Hints

Data structure

```
@letters = ['U', 'K', 'S', 'A', 'R', 'G', 'I', 'N']
@letter_to_digits = {} # hash store the solution
@is_digit_used = {0 => false, 1 => false, 2 => false, 3 => false, 4 => false, 5 => false,\
 6 => false, 7 => false, 8 => false, 9 => false }
```

@letters is defined as an array, so that we can start trying first letter @letters[0], then @letters[1], ..., etc.

@letter_to_digits stores possible combinations, e.g. @letter_to_digits["U"] => 9; @letter_to_digits["A"] => 1;

@is_digit_used is used to ensure that a digit can only be assigned to one letter.

Decode letters to digits

Decode a string to return a number based on the each character's corresponding integer. For example, decode_letters_to_number("USA", {"U" => 1, "K" => 4, "S" => 3, "A" => 2}) returns number 132.

```
def decode_letters_to_number(letter_string, letter_to_digit_lookup)
  # ...
end
```

Check answer

This is to verify whether a possible combination satisfies the equation.

```
def check_ans()
  uk = decode_letters_to_number('UK', letter_to_digit_lookup)
  # ...
  # print out the solution if uk + usa + ussr == aging
end
```

10.6 More Puzzle Exercises

Here are some more fun puzzles that are great for programming exercises.

Tower of Hanoi

The objective of the game is to move all the disks onto a different pole.

1. Only one disk can be moved at a time.
2. Each move consists of taking the upper disk from one of the stacks and placing it on top of another stack i.e. a disk can only be moved if it is the uppermost disk on a stack.
3. No disk can be placed on top of a smaller disk.

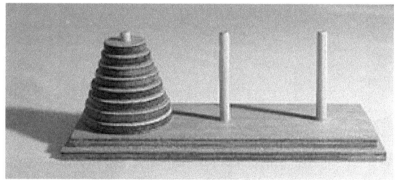

(source: wikipedia[2])

Knight's tour

A knight's tour is a sequence of moves of a knight on a chessboard such that the knight visits every square exactly once.

---

[2]http://en.wikipedia.org/wiki/Tower_of_Hanoi

(source: wikipedia[3])

Eight Queens puzzle

Place eight chess queens on an 8x8 chessboard so that no queens is attacking any of the others, that is, no two queens share the same row, column and diagonal.

(source: wikipedia[4])

---

[3]http://en.wikipedia.org/wiki/Knight%27s_tour
[4]http://en.wikipedia.org/wiki/Eight_queens_puzzle

11. Web Test Automation

Web Test Automation, or automated functional testing for web applications via the Graphical User Interface (GUI), is the use of automated test scripts to drive test executions to verify that the web application meets requirements. To put it simply, during the execution of an automated test for a website, you see mouse and keyboard actions such as clicking a button and typing text in a text box in a browser, without human intervention. Those actions were driven by test scripts.

To effectively develop automated test scripts, mastering programming is a must. Ruby is regarded as the best language for writing test scripts. In this chapter, we will use Ruby script to test web applications.

11.1 The best job is not far away

Before we start, let's see an article on Forbes[1].

> ### The Happiest Jobs In America: software quality assurance engineer
>
> The happiest job of all isn't kindergarten teacher or dentist. It's software quality assurance engineer. Professionals with this job title are typically involved in the entire software development process to ensure the quality of the final product. This can include processes such as requirements gathering and documentation, source code control, code review, change management, configuration management, release management, and the actual testing of the software, explains Matt Miller, chief technology officer at CareerBliss.
>
> With an index score of 4.24, software quality assurance engineers said they are more than satisfied with the people they work with and the company they work for. They're also fairly content with their daily tasks and bosses.
>
> These professionals "typically make between $85,000 and $100,000 a year in salary and are the gatekeepers for releasing high quality software products," Miller says. Organizations generally will not allow software to be released until it has been fully tested and approved by their software quality assurance group, he adds.

---

[1] http://www.forbes.com/sites/jacquelynsmith/2012/03/23/the-happiest-jobs-in-america

Happiest Jobs in America

Rank	Job Title	Bliss Rating	Average Salary	All Available Jobs
1	Software Quality Assurance Engineer	4.245	$66,403	View Jobs (75556)
2	Executive Chef	4.152	$58,735	View Jobs (3338)
3	Property Manager	4.147	$49,034	View Jobs (39914)

The happiest job list in USA[a]

[a]"http://www.careerbliss.com/facts-and-figures/happiest-and-unhappiest-jobs-17/"

The advantages of being software testers for web applications.

- **Big demand**

  Now a large percentage of new software development are web applications. There are also considerable legacy desktop applications will be migrated to web-based. Comparing to traditional desktop client development, web applications (or as a result of modern software development practices) require far more frequent releases. As a result, a lot more testing effort is needed. Furthermore, the emerging requirement of supporting all leading browsers: IE, Chrome and Firefox also means demanding more testing resources.

- **Relatively stable skill set**

  Some IT professionals left this industry because the technologies change too quickly, this is particularly true for programmers. I have been working in IT over 18 years, seeing many technologies come and go. However, the skill set for testing web applications is relatively stable. While there are advancements in web technologies, the fundamental and core ones such as HTML, CSS and JavaScripts remain largely the same.

- **Transferable skill**

  The knowledge and experience you gained at company A is directly applicable to company B, as long as you are testing web applications.

- **Few possess the skills**

  We know that there is no degree in software testing, and I never heard of any universities offering courses in automated testing (This puzzles me. We all know that software tester is an essential role in software projects). As a result, very few people possess test automation knowledge.

A good news for you, the knowledge you gained from doing this book's exercises plus some extra effort (see below) will put you in a position well ahead of your peers, if you are interested in getting 'the happiest job in USA'.

11.2 Drive Firefox with Selenium WebDriver

Selenium WebDriver is the most popular testing framework for web and mobile applications. There is clearly trend that more and more software companies, such as Facebook, desire Selenium skills from programmers and software test engineers. Selenium supports all major browsers and tests can be written in many programming languages and run on Windows, Linux and Macintosh platforms.

Install Selenium WebDriver

```
gem install selenium-webdriver
```

If you use Windows, `selenium-webdriver` gem is already included RubyShell.

Sample Selenium-WebDriver Script

```
require 'selenium-webdriver'

browser = Selenium::WebDriver.for(:chrome)
browser.navigate.to("http://travel.agileway.net")

browser.find_element(:id, "username").send_keys("agileway")
browser.find_element(:id, "password").send_keys("testwise")
browser.find_element(:xpath,"//input[@value='Sign in']").click

browser.find_elements(:name => "tripType").each { |elem| elem.click && break if elem.attr\
ibute("value") == "oneway" && elem.attribute("type") == "radio" }

 # one way of using select in selenium: slow
select_elem = browser.find_element(:name, "fromPort");
options = select_elem.find_elements(:tag_name, "option");
options.each { |opt| opt.click if opt.text == "New York"}

Selenium::WebDriver::Support::Select.new(browser.find_element(:name, "toPort")).select_by\
(:text, "Sydney")
```

```
Selenium::WebDriver::Support::Select.new(browser.find_element(:id, "departDay")).select_b\
y(:text, "04")
Selenium::WebDriver::Support::Select.new(browser.find_element(:id, "departMonth")).select\
_by(:text, "March 2012")
browser.find_element(:xpath,"//input[@value='Continue']").click

browser.find_element(:name, "passengerFirstName").send_keys("Wise")
browser.find_element(:name, "passengerLastName").send_keys("Tester")
browser.find_element(:xpath,"//input[@value='Next']").click

browser.find_elements(:name => "card_type").each { |elem| elem.click && break if elem.att\
ribute("value") == "visa" && elem.attribute("type") == "radio" }
browser.find_element(:name, "card_number").send_keys("4000000000000000")
Selenium::WebDriver::Support::Select.new(browser.find_element(:name, "expiry_year")).sele\
ct_by(:text, "2013")
browser.find_element(:xpath,"//input[@value='Pay now']").click
```

11.3 Drive Chrome with Selenium WebDriver

Selenium requires **chomedriver** to be installed, and put in the system **PATH**.

1. Download chromedriver[2]. The current version is 2.32.
2. Add to PATH
   - Windows
     Edit "PATH" in "Environment Variables".
   - Mac or Linux
     ```
     cp ~/Downloads/chromedriver /usr/local/bin
     ```

Now run the script. You will see it running in Chrome.

11.4 Complete Test with Verification

Web test drivers such as Watir and Selenium WebDriver drive browsers. However, to make effective use of them for testing, we need put them in a test framework which defines test structures and provides assertions (performing checks in test scripts after 'driving' the application to a certain point).

In the context of web testing, typical checks are:

---
[2]https://sites.google.com/a/chromium.org/chromedriver/downloads

- verify certain texts are present
- verify page title
- verify a link is present
- verify a web control is present or hidden

RSpec

RSpec is a popular test framework in Ruby. Standard gem installation (`gem install rspec`) or using RubyShell. The below is a complete test script in RSpec.

```
require 'selenium-webdriver'
require 'rspec'

describe "Book flight" do

  before(:all) do
    @browser = $browser = Selenium::WebDriver.for(:firefox)
    @browser.navigate.to("http://travel.agileway.net")
  end

  after(:all) do
    @browser.quit
  end

  it "Book flight with payment" do
    @browser.find_element(:id, "username").send_keys("agileway")
    @browser.find_element(:id, "password").send_keys("testwise")
    @browser.find_element(:xpath,"//input[@value='Sign in']").click
    # check whether signed in OK?
    expect(@browser.page_source).to include("Signed in!")

    @browser.find_elements(:name => "tripType").each { |elem| elem.click && break if elem\
.attribute("value") == "oneway" && elem.attribute("type") == "radio" }

    Selenium::WebDriver::Support::Select.new(@browser.find_element(:name, "fromPort")).se\
lect_by(:text, "New York")
    Selenium::WebDriver::Support::Select.new(@browser.find_element(:name, "toPort")).sele\
ct_by(:text, "Sydney")
    Selenium::WebDriver::Support::Select.new(@browser.find_element(:id, "departDay")).sel\
ect_by(:text, "04")
    Selenium::WebDriver::Support::Select.new(@browser.find_element(:id, "departMonth")).s\
```

```
elect_by(:text, "March 2012")

    @browser.find_element(:xpath,"//input[@value='Continue']").click
    @browser.find_element(:name, "passengerFirstName").send_keys("Wise")
    @browser.find_element(:name, "passengerLastName").send_keys("Tester")
    @browser.find_element(:xpath,"//input[@value='Next']").click

    @browser.find_element(:xpath, "//input[@name='card_type' and @value='visa']").click
    @browser.find_element(:name, "card_number").send_keys("4000000000000000")
    select_elem = @browser.find_element(:name, "expiry_year");
    options = select_elem.find_elements(:tag_name, "option");
    options.each { |opt| opt.click if opt.text == "2013"}
    @browser.find_element(:xpath,"//input[@value='Pay now']").click

    sleep 10
    # check receipt info
    expect(@browser.page_source).to include("2012-03-04   <b>New York</b> to <b>Sydney</b\
>")
  end

end
```

Besides the test statements driving the application, it contains two checks:

- verify that user signed in OK, after clicking 'Sign in' button
- verify that final receipt page (after payment) contains flight details

```
# ...
expect(@browser.page_source).to include("Signed in!")
# ...
expect(@browser.page_source).to include("2012-03-04   <b>New York</b> to <b>Sydney</b>")
```

11.5 For more on test automation ...

Obviously, here we have only touched the very basic of test automation for web applications. The messages I am trying to convey in the chapter:

- You can use Ruby to do some real work, or get a promising career.
- You understand test scripts now, and probably can write some of your own.

If you are interested in test automation, please check the resources section for more.

12. Beyond This Book

If you look back the time when you started the first exercise, you probably realize that you have learned a lot. While this book stops here, your learning won't. You have just laid a good foundation to achieve more with computer, with the power of programming.

12.1 More Ruby

We have covered the fundamentals of Ruby. To know more cool features of Ruby, such as Blocks, I would highly recommend the book: "Programming Ruby 1.9 & 2.0: The Pragmatic Programmers' Guide"[1]. It is commonly known as "The PickAxe" because of the pickaxe illustration on the cover. Ruby programming language was created by Yukihiro Matsumoto ("Matz") in Japan, "The PickAxe" has helped Ruby to spread outside Japan[2].

12.2 More exercises

Programming is just like any other skills, more practices will make it better. As computers are part of our life, if you pay attention, you will find a lot areas that you can apply your programming skills to. For example, some exercises in this book are from my daughter's Math homework.

Even you cannot think of something now, try redo some exercises by adding variations, especially those ones that you had troubles with for the first time.

12.3 Automated Testing with Ruby

If you have completed all the exercises, you will have enough programming skills required for a good automated tester (2012's the happiest job in USA according to this Forbes report[3], the second in both 2013 and 2014). As a matter of fact, one of the reasons of writing this book

---

[1]https://pragprog.com/book/ruby4/programming-ruby-1-9-2-0
[2]http://www.infoq.com/interviews/david-black
[3]http://www.forbes.com/sites/jacquelynsmith/2012/03/23/the-happiest-jobs-in-america

is to respond the question I received from the readers of my other book *Practical Web Test Automation*: "Can you recommend a book on Ruby?"

Ruby, in my opinion, is the most suitable script language for writing automated tests. The over 10 million downloads of Selenium-WebDriver (the most popular web testing library, used in Facebook and Google) Ruby gem supports my view.

12.4 Web Programming with Ruby on Rails

Many people heard of Ruby the first time from the term "Ruby on Rails", a popular web application framework written in Ruby. Many large web sites running Ruby on Rails include Hulu, Shopify, Yammer, Scribd and GitHub. Besides large web sites, Ruby on Rails is very popular in startups.

The word "Web" in web programming means you also need master web technologies, such as

- HTML
- JavaScripts
- Cascading Style Sheets (CSS)

Codecademy[4] offers free courses for the above.

Rails Resources:

- Book: Agile Web Development with Rails 4[5] - the definite guide to Ruby on Rails development.
- ScreenCasts: RailsCasts[6] - great Rails tutorial screencast by Ryan Bates.
- Online Course: Codecademy's Make a Rails App course[7]

Recommended Rails exercise

If you don't have a web project in mind, I suggest implementing a library system (extended from ex9-4) in Rails. In the ex9-4, this over-simplified library system has three features:

---

[4]http://www.codecademy.com/
[5]"https://pragprog.com/book/rails4/agile-web-development-with-rails-4"
[6]http://railscasts.com/
[7]http://www.codecademy.com/en/learn/make-a-rails-app/

- Import books into the system
- Borrow a book
- Return a book

Of course, they need to be rewritten in Rails (not hard to do). Then you can add more features:

- Register new member
- Register a new book
- Member can login (see RailsCasts for episodes on user authentication)
- Member can view borrowing history
- Library staff send due date reminders
- Member can renew
- ...

It is common that beginners plan big and rush to coding, end up too complex to handle. The proper way is to start simple and enhance the system gradually.

Also it is a good idea to write some automated tests for your web application. You might be surprised that how useful they are.

Web applications developed by me

- **ClinicWise**[a], a web-based health practice management system.
- **BuildWise**[b], a Continuous Testing server with good support in executing automated UI tests.
- **SiteWise CMS**[c], a content management system (CMS) to build dynamic web sites.
- **AdminWise**, a web application manages administration tasks including a library system.

[a]https://clinicwise.net/
[b]https://testwisely.com/buildwise
[c]http://sitewisecms.com/

12.5 Game Programming and Mobile Apps

Comparing to other main-stream programming languages such as Java and C#, Ruby lacks behind on Graphical User Interface (GUI) support, maybe due to the majority use of Ruby are either web application development (Rails) or scripting (automated testing). Having said that, it is possible to write desktop applications in Ruby. For example, I developed Testwise, a testing IDE, in Ruby.

Besides web applications, the other main focus of software development is on iOS or Android apps. RubyMotion[8] is a commercial product (you need to pay after free trial) that lets you develop cross-platform native apps for iOS, Android and OS X in Ruby.

12.6 Learn another programming language

It is common that a programmer needs to master several programming languages. As I said in the preface, once you have mastered one programming language, it is easy to learn another. If you like the format of this book, you may want to get my second book in "Learn Programming by examples series": Learn Swift by Examples[9].

---

[8]"http://www.rubymotion.com/"
[9]https://leanpub.com/learn-swift-programming-by-examples

Appendix 1 Ruby in Nutshell

A quick summary of core Ruby syntax in code examples.

Print out

```ruby
# print out text
puts "a" + "b";          # => "ab"
puts 1 + 2;                 # => 3
puts "1" + "2";             # => "12"

# print out without new line after
print "Hi"
print "Bob"
# the screen output will be "HiBob"

# print out joined multiple strings
print "Bye", " John"    # => "Bye John"
```

Variable assignment

```ruby
total = 1 + 2 + 3;   # => total has value: 6
average = total / 3;
puts average;              # => 2

## print string with variable
puts "total is " + total.to_s
puts "average is #{average}"
```

Read user input

```
input = gets          # => type "Hi"
puts input            # => "Hi\n"

## normally strip off the new line "\n"
input = gets.chomp  # => "Hi"

## read an integer
print "Enter a number"
num = gets.chomp.to_i
```

Conditional

Two boolean values: true and false

if

```
if score < 0
  score = 0  # no negative score
end
```

unless

```
unless score >= 0
  score = 0  # no negative score
end
```

Single line if and unless

```
puts "Warning: close to limit" if user_count > 10
puts "Warning: close to limit" if user_count <= 10
```

if, elsif and else

```
if true
  puts "OK"
else
  puts "Never reach here"
end


a = 10
b = 20
if a > b
  puts "a is bigger"
elsif a < b
  puts "b is bigger"
else
  puts "a,b the same"
end
```

Case and When

```
score = 70

result = case score
   when 0..60
     "Fail"
   when 61..70
      "Pass"
   when 71..95
     "Pass with Distinction"
   when 96, 97, 98, 99
     "Distinction"
   when 100
     "High Distinction"
   else
     "Invalid Score"
   end
puts result # => Pass
```

Looping

1. **while** loop

```
count = 0
while count < 10
 count = count + 1
 print count, " "
end
# 1 2 3 4 5 6 7 8 9
```

2. **for** loop

```
for i in 1..9
   print i, " "
end
# 1 2 3 4 5 6 7 8 9
```

3. **until** loop

```
count = 1
until count >=  5
   print count, " "
   count +=1
end
# 1 2 3 4
```

4. **times** loop

```
number = 2
3.times do
   number = number * number
end
# 3 calculations: 2 * 2, 4 * 4, 16 * 16
puts number # => 256
```

Skip to next loop: next

Ignore this remaining statements in the current loop, start the next loop.

```
(1..5).each do |num|
  puts "Checking #{num} ..."
  next if num % 2 != 0    # Skip odd numbers
  puts "#{num} is an even number."
end
```

Output:

```
Checking 1 ...
Checking 2 ...
2 is an even number.
Checking 3 ...
Checking 4 ...
4 is an even number.
Checking 5 ...
```

Exit a loop: break

```
while input = gets.chomp
  puts input
  if input == "exit"
    break
  end
end
```

Infinite loop

```
while true
  # the code within will be running again and again
  # you shall really add an exit condition
end
```

Array

```
score_list = [20, 10, 30, 50]
score_list.size # => 4
score_list.reverse        # => [50, 30, 10, 20]
score_list.sort             # => [10,20,30,50], score_list itself not changed
puts score_list            # =>           [20, 10, 30, 50]
score_list.sort!            ## change itself
puts score_list            # =>           [10, 20, 30, 50]
```

Accessing array element

```
most_spoken_langs = ["Chinese", "Spanish", "English", "Hindi", "Arabic"]
most_spoken_langs[0] # => "Chinese", indexing starts 0
most_spoken_langs[2] # => "English"
most_spoken_langs[-1]   # => "Arabic",  last one
most_spoken_langs[-2]   # => "Hindi"
most_spoken_langs.include?("Spanish")   # => true
most_spoken_langs.include?("Italian")   # => false
```

Add and remove array elements

```
score_list = [20, 10, 30, 50]
score_list.delete(30)                 # score_list will be [[20, 10, 50]
score_list << 90
score_list << 80
puts score_list        # => [20, 10, 50, 90, 80]
```

Iterate an array

```
[20, 10, 30].each do |elem|
  puts "Square of #{elem} is #{elem * elem}"
end
```

Output:

```
Square of 20 is 400
Square of 10 is 100
Square of 30 is 900
```

Hash

Initialize, add and delete Hash elements

```
us_states = {"CA" => "California", "NY" => "New York", "TX" => "Texas"}
us_states["FL"] = "Florida"
us_states.size # => 4
us_states.delete("NY")
puts us_states.inspect #=> {"CA"=>"California","TX"=>"Texas","FL"=>"Florida"}
```

Iterate a Hash

```
us_states.each { |key, value|
  puts "#{value}'s abbreviation is " + key
}
```

Output:

```
California's abbreviation is CA
Texas's abbreviation is TX
Florida's abbreviation is FL
```

Method

```
def square(num)
  num * num    # => equal to return num * num
end

puts square(2)  # => 4
puts square(9)  # => 81
```

Method arguments with default values

```
def exponent(num, power = 2)
  num ** power  ## exponential calculation
end

exponent(5)     # => 25
exponent(5, 3)  # => 125
```

Scope

```ruby
@c = 1        # @instance variable, scope of file

def add(a, b)
  c = a + b # local scope of function
  @c  = c   # set instance variable's value
  puts "inside c = #{c}"
end

c = 100;     # local scope of outside, different from the c in add()
add(1, 2)
puts "outside c = #{c}"
puts "instance variable @c = #{@c}"
```

Output:

```
inside c = 3
outside c = 100
instance variable @c = 3
```

Nested Loop

```ruby
# times table
for i in 1..9 do
  for j in 1..9 do
        puts "#{i}x#{j} = #{i*j}"
      end
end
```

Class

```ruby
class Bird
  def fly
    puts "I am flying"
  end
end

class Seagull < Bird
end

class Parrot < Bird
  def speak
    puts "if someone teaches me"
  end
end

seagull = Seagull.new
seagull.fly   # => "I am flying"

parrot = Parrot.new
parrot.fly    # => "I am flying"
parrot.speak  # => "if someone teaches me"

class Ostrich < Bird
  def fly
              puts "I rather run"
  end
end

ostrich = Ostrich.new
ostrich.fly #=> "I rather run"

seagull.speak # NoMethodError: undefined method `speak' for #<Seagull:xxx>
```

Module and Mixin

```ruby
module Logging

  def log(message)
    puts "[#{Time.now}] [#{self.class.name}] #{message}"
  end

end

class A
  include Logging
end

class B
  include Logging
end

class C
end

a = A.new
b = B.new
c = C.new

a.log("in A") # => [2014-11-08 16:07:32 +1000] [A] in A
b.log("in A") # => [2014-11-08 16:07:32 +1000] [B] in B
c.log("in C") # => undefined method `log' for #<C:0x007fdbfa075480> (NoMethodError)
```

File I/O

Read file

```ruby
file_path = File.join(File.dirname(__FILE__), "files", "score.txt")
file_content = File.read(file_path)
```

Write to file

```
# to append existing file, use 'a' instead of 'w'
fio = File.open("c:/tmp/output.txt", "w")
fio.puts("string to write into file")
fio.close
```

Date

```
require 'date' # need to load first
# assume today is 2014-11-25
Date.today.to_s   # => "2014-11-07"
Date.today.class  # => Date
Date.today.year   = 2014
Date.today.month = 11
Date.today.day    = 25

Date.parse("2014-01-29") # => a date object
```

Appendix 2 Solutions

Chapter 2

2.1 Print out Triangle

```
10.times do |count|
  # count starts with 0 then 1, 2, 3 ...
  puts "*" * (count + 1)
end
```

Ruby's `times` do can optionally pass the looping index to the code within the block, the looping index starts with 0.

```
10.times do |looping_index|
  # ...
end
```

2.2 Print out a half diamond

```
15.times do |row|
  # row starting with 0
  if row < 8
    star_count  = row + 1
  else
    star_count  = (15 - row)
  end
  puts '*' * star_count
end
```

2.3 Print out diamond shape

```
15.times do |row|
  if row < 8
  star_count  = row * 2 + 1
  space_count = 8 - row
  else
  star_count  = (15 - row) * 2 - 1
  space_count  = row - 6
  end
  puts ' ' * space_count + '*' * star_count
end
```

2.4 Print big diamond, name your size

```
print "Enter the maximum number of rows (odd number):"
size = gets.chomp.to_i
space = " "
space_count = size / 2 + 1 # initial space count for first row
middle_row = size / 2 + 1
size.times do |row|
  if row < middle_row
    space_count -= 1
    star_count  = row * 2 + 1
  else
    space_count += 1
    star_count  = (size - 1 - row) * 2 + 1
  end
  print space * space_count
  puts '*' * star_count
end
```

Some minor enhancements over Courtney's:

- puts will start a new line, so I used print to print out the static text for asking user's input.
- introduce variable middle_row to improve code readability. In fact, Courtney got failure initially because did not update the if row < ... condition correctly.
- move print space * space_count out of if statements (duplication)

Chapter 3

3.1 Simple Add Calculator

```
puts "I am an Adding Machine and I am good at it"
puts "Enter first number:"
num1 = gets.chomp.to_i
puts "Enter second number:"
num2 = gets.chomp.to_i
puts "Thinking..."
answer = num1 + num2
puts "Got it, the answer is: #{answer}"
```

3.2 Addition Quiz

```
count = 0
10.times do
  num1 = rand(10)
  num2 = rand(10)
  print "#{num1} + #{num2} ="
  answer = num1 + num2
  input = gets.chomp.to_i
  if answer == input
    puts "Correct!"
    count += 1
  else
    puts "Wrong!"
  end
end
puts "Your score is #{count}/10"
```

Courtney forgot the "You score: " part, which she added later.

3.3 Subtraction Quiz

```
count = 0
10.times do
  num1 = rand(10)
  num2 = rand(10)
  if num1 > num2
      print "#{num1} - #{num2} = "
      answer = num1 - num2
  else
      print "#{num2} - #{num1} = "
      answer = num2 - num1
  end
  input = gets.chomp.to_i
  if answer == input
    puts "Correct!"
    count = count += 1
  else
    puts "Wrong!"
  end
end
puts "Your score is #{count}/10"
```

3.4 Number Guessing Game

```
puts "I have a secret number (0-9) Can you guess it?"
count = 0
the_secret_number = rand(10)
while input = gets.chomp.to_i
  count += 1
  if input > the_secret_number
    puts "TOO BIG"
  elsif input < the_secret_number
    puts "too small"
  else
    puts "CORRECT"
    break
  end
end
puts "The number is : #{the_secret_number}. and you guessed #{count} times!!"
```

Chapter 4

4.1 Sort Children Names

```
array = []
input = nil
puts "Enter child names in class: (0 to finish)"
until input == "0"
  input = gets.chomp
  if input != "0"
    array << input
  end
end
puts "Kids in order:"
puts array.sort.join(", ")
```

4.2 Get the character from given alphabetical position

```
array = ["A", "B", "C", "D", "E", "F", "G", "H", "I", "J", "K", "L", "M", "N", "O", "P", \
"Q", "R", "S", "T", "U", "V", "W", "X", "Y", "Z"]
puts "I know the alphabet very well, enter the alphabetical order number (integer) and I \
will tell you the corresponding letter, 0 to quit:"

while true
  input = gets.chomp.to_i
  if input == 0
    break
  end
  n = input - 1
  puts array[n]
end
```

The above use `while` infinite loop, you may also use `until` loop as below:

```
until (input = gets.chomp.to_i) == 0
  n = input - 1
  puts array[n]
end
```

4.3 Calculate Average

```
array = []
count = 0
puts "Enter scores: "
while true
  input = gets.chomp.to_i
  break if input == -1

  array << input
  count += 1
end
the_sum = array.inject{|sum,x| sum + x }
average = the_sum / count
puts "Average score: #{average}"
```

4.4 What makes 100% in life?

```
alpha_value_lookups = {}
%w(A B C D E F G H I J K L M N O P Q R S T U V W X Y Z).each_with_index do |ch, idx|
  alpha_value_lookups[ch] = idx + 1
end
print "Enter word in capitals: "
input = gets.chomp

the_value = 0
input.split("").each do |character|
  the_value += alpha_value_lookups[character]
end

puts "The value of meaning to life: #{the_value}%"
```

I constructed the hash look-up from an alphabetical array. There are other ways too. Here I will show you three things

- initialize an array using %w(STRING1 STRING2 ...)
- relationship and difference between an array and a hash
- each_with_index to pass loop indexing (starting from 0) to the block code within the loop

Courtney used the array to sum the value, which is not necessary.

Chapter 5

5.1 Fahrenheit to Celsius Converter

```
print "Enter temperature in Fahrenheit: "
input = gets.chomp.to_f
celsius = (input - 32) * 5 / 9.0
print "In Celsius: "
puts celsius.round(2)
```

5.2 Personal Income Tax Calculator

```
puts "Enter your annual income: "
income = gets.chomp.to_i

tax = 0

case income
when 0..18200
  puts "No tax"
when 18201..37000
  tax = (income - 18200) * 0.19
when 37001..80000
  tax = (income - 37000) * 0.325 + 3572
when 37001..80000
  tax = (income - 87000) * 0.37 + 19822
else
  tax = (income - 180000) * 0.45 + 54232
end
tax = tax.round(2)
puts "Your personal income tax amount: $#{tax}"
```

Using case statement.

```
# read income as integer
case income
when 0..18200
  puts "No tax"
when 18201..37000
  tax = (income - 18200) * 0.19
when 37001..80000
  tax = (income - 37000) * 0.325 + 3572
when 80001..180000
  tax = (income - 80000) * 0.37 + 17547
else
  tax = (income - 180000) * 0.45 + 54547
end
```

5.3 Word count

```
str = 'Practical Web Test Automation' book is great. The end.'
puts "The text has #{str.split(' ').size} words"
```

5.4 Generate Lotto Numbers

```
count = 0
array = []
until count == 6
  lotto_number = rand(49)
  lotto_number += 1
  if array.include?(lotto_number)
    # puts "ALREADY HAS #{lotto_number}"
  next
  else
    array << lotto_number
    count += 1
  end
end
puts "Your winning lotto numbers are #{array}, good luck!"
```

5.5 Number sorting

```
array = [10, 8, 7, 3, 4, 5, 9, 1, 2, 6]
array.each_with_index do |num, idx|
  # puts "num = #{num}"
  # puts "idx = #{idx}"

  # comparing No.idx with remaining ones
  (idx+1..array.size() - 1).each do |idx2|
    if array[idx] > array[idx2]
      # swap
      array[idx], array[idx2] = array[idx2], array[idx]
    end
  end
end
puts "The numbers in order: #{array.join(', ')}"
```

Chapter 6

6.1 Finding Divisors

```
check = nil
array = []
print "Enter a number: "
input = gets.chomp.to_i
(1..input).each do |x|
  check = input % x
  if check == 0
    array << x
  end
end
puts "The divisors of #{input}: #{array.join(", ")}"
```

6.2 Finding the Highest Common Factor

```ruby
divisors_list_1 = []
divisors_list_2 = []
puts "Enter first number: "
num1 = gets.chomp.to_i
(1..num1).each do |x|
  check = num1 % x
  if check == 0
    divisors_list_1 << x
  end
end
puts "Enter second number: "
num2 = gets.chomp.to_i
(1..num2).each do |x|
  check = num2 % x
  if check == 0
    divisors_list_2 << x
  end
end

d1sorted = divisors_list_1.sort.reverse
d1sorted.each do |elem|
  # puts "elem = #{elem}"
  if divisors_list_2.include?(elem)
    puts "The HCF is #{elem}"
    break
  end
end
```

6.3 Finding the Least Common Multiple (LCM)

```ruby
puts "Enter the first number: "
num1 = gets.chomp.to_i
puts "Enter the second number:"
num2 = gets.chomp.to_i
if num1 > num2
  check = num1
else
  check = num2
end
puts "check = #{check}"
start_time = Time.now
(check..num1 * num2).step(check) do |n|
```

```
 #   puts "n % num1 = #{n % num1}"
 #   puts "n % num2 = #{n % num2}"
 if n % num1 == 0 && n % num2 == 0
   puts "The LCM for #{num1} and #{num2} is #{n}"
   break
 end
end
puts "Calculation took #{Time.now - start_time} seconds"
```

6.4 Finding Prime Numbers

```
array = []
(2..20).each do |num|
  # check one number is a prime number or not
  flag = true
  (2..num - 1).each do |x| # trying to check each possible divisor
    if num % x == 0
      flag = false # mark this has divisor
      break # no point to check more - composite, moves on to next
    end
  end
  if flag == true  # the number has no divisors
    array << num # add to prime number list
  end
end
puts "Prime numbers (up to 20) are : #{array.join(', ')}"
```

6.5 Fibonacci sequence

```
array = [1, 1]
num1 = 1
num2 = 1
10.times do
  next_number = num1 + num2
  array << next_number
  num1 = num2
  num2 = next_number
end
puts "The number of rabbit pairs are: #{array.join(', ')}"
```

6.6 Consecutive Sums

```
print "Enter a number: "
x = gets.chomp.to_i
y = (x + 1) / 2
(1..y-1).each do |starting_number|
  #  puts "starting num = #{starting_number}"
  (starting_number..y).each do |j|
    # puts "j = #{j}"
    sum = (starting_number..j).to_a.inject(0){|sum, item| sum + item}
    if sum == x
      puts "#{x} = #{(starting_number..j).to_a.join(' + ')}"
    end
  end
end
```

Chapter 7

7.1 Finding the Highest Common Factor (using method)

```
def get_divisors(num)
  array = []
  (1..num).each do |x|
    check = num % x
    if check == 0
      array << x
    end
  end
  return array
end

puts "Enter first number: "
num1 = gets.chomp.to_i
divisors_list_1 = get_divisors(num1)

puts "Enter second number: "
num2 = gets.chomp.to_i
divisors_list_2 = get_divisors(num2)

d1sorted = divisors_list_1.sort.reverse
d1sorted.each do |elem|
  if divisors_list_2.include?(elem)
    puts "The HCF is #{elem}"
    break
  end
end
```

7.2 Generate Lotto Numbers (using method)

```
def get_next_valid_lotto_number(existing_lotto_numbers)
  new_lotto_number = rand(49)
  while existing_lotto_numbers.include?(new_lotto_number)
  new_lotto_number = rand(49)
  end
  return new_lotto_number
end

lotto_numbers = []
6.times do
  new_valid_number = get_next_valid_lotto_number(lotto_numbers)
  lotto_numbers << new_valid_number
end
```

```
puts "Your winning lotto numbers are #{lotto_numbers.inspect}, good luck!"
```

7.3 Finding the LCM for multiple numbers (using method)

```
# a function returns lcm for a and b
def lcm(a, b)
  (a..a*b).each do |n|
    if n % a == 0 && n % b == 0
      # puts "n = #{n}"
      return n
      next
    end # end of if
  end # end of loop
end

# trying out functions
# m = lcm(1, 2)
# m = lcm(m, 3)

m = 1
(2..15).each do |w|
  m = lcm(m, w)
  # puts "The LCM for up to #{w} is #{m}"
end
puts "The lowest number that is dividable by 1 to 15 is: #{m}"
```

Chapter 8

8.1 Calculate average score

```
file = File.join(File.dirname(__FILE__), "files", "score.txt")
file_content =  File.read(file)

array = []
file_content.split("\n").each do |line|
   array << line.to_i
end

the_sum = array.inject{|sum,x| sum + x }
the_average = the_sum * 1.0 / array.size
the_average = the_average.round(1)
puts "Average score is #{the_average}"
```

8.2 Count words and lines in a text file

Write a program that reads the contents of a file and counts the number of words and lines in that file.

```
ruby count_words_and_lines.rb file.txt
file.txt contains 126 words in 13 lines
```

Solution

```
first_command_line_argument = ARGV[0]

input_file_path =  File.join(".", first_command_line_argument)
input_file_full_path = File.expand_path(input_file_path)

file_content = File.read(input_file_full_path)

word_count = file_content.split.size
line_count = file_content.split("\n").size

puts "#{first_command_line_argument} contains #{word_count} words in #{line_count} lines"
```

8.3 Mail merge birthday invitation cards

```ruby
guest_list = ["Pokkle", "Angela", "Tonpa", "Toby", "Biscuit", "Mito", "Kate", "Renee", "C\
hloe", "Kelly", "Melody"]

invitation = "Dear {{first_name}},

I am celebrating my 12th Birthday on the 1st of April!
Come celebrate with me!

Where: 42 Greed-Island Street, Yorkshin City
When: 2PM to 5PM
RSVP: 24th of March (0400-000-000 or rsvpjessica@gmail.com)

Hope to see you there,

Jessica."

guest_list.each do |name|
  named_invitation = invitation.gsub("{{first_name}}", name)
  puts named_invitation
  File.open("C:\\Users\\you\\rubycode\\#{name.downcase}_invitation.txt", "w").write(named\
_invitation)
end
```

8.4 Rename files

```ruby
require 'fileutils'
directory = File.expand_path( File.join(File.dirname(__FILE__), "files", "book_dir"))

Dir.foreach(directory) do |item|
  next if item == '.' or item == '..'
  # puts item
  if item =~ /chapter\s(\d+)(.*)/
    sequence = $1
    new_sequence = $1.rjust(2, "0")
    new_filename = "chapter_" + new_sequence + $2
    # puts new_filename
    FileUtils.mv(File.join(directory, item), File.join(directory, new_filename))
  end
end
```

8.5 Currency exchange with life quoting

```ruby
require 'net/http'
require 'uri'

def get_url_content(url)
  begin
    url_content =   Net::HTTP.get(URI.parse(url))
    return url_content
  rescue => e
    puts "Unable to connect to Yahoo Finance, Error: '#{e}'"
    exit(-1)
  end
end


def retrieve_exchange_rate_yahoo_csv
  require 'csv'
  csv_data = get_url_content("http://download.finance.yahoo.com/d/quotes.csv?s=AUDJPY=X&f\
=sl1d1t1ba&e=.csv")
  csv = CSV.parse(csv_data) # CSV.
  csv_first_row =  csv.shift
  exchange_rate = csv_first_row[1].to_f
end



def retrieve_exchange_rate_currencyconverterapi_json
  require 'json'
  json_str = get_url_content("https://free.currencyconverterapi.com/api/v5/convert?q=AUD_\
JPY&compact=y")
  json_obj = JSON.parse(json_str)
  return json_obj["AUD_JPY"]["val"].to_f
end

print "Enter the amount of Australian dollars: "
exchange_rate = retrieve_exchange_rate_currencyconverterapi_json
aud_amount = gets.chomp.to_f
jpy_amount = (aud_amount * exchange_rate).round(2)
puts "=> ¥ #{jpy_amount}"
```

8.6 Send individual thank you emails

```
test_mode = true

my_email = "me@gmail.com" # change to yours

guest_list = [
  {:first_name => "Pokkle", :email => "pokkle@archer.com", :gift => "Bow and Arrows"},
  {:first_name => "Angela", :email => "catlover@gmail.com", :gift => "Cat Statue"},
  # ...
]

thank_you_template = "Dear {{first_name}},

Thank you for coming to my 12th party, I really like the gift you gave me: {{gift}}, than\
k you very much!

Jessica"

require 'mail'

options = {
   :enable_starttls_auto => true,
   :address => 'smtp.gmail.com',
   :port => 587,
   :authentication => 'plain',
   :user_name => 'yourname@gmail.com',
   :password => 'secret'
}

Mail.defaults do
   delivery_method :smtp, options
end

guest_list.each do |entry|
  content = thank_you_template.gsub("{{first_name}}", entry[:first_name]).gsub("{{gift}}"\
, entry[:gift])

  puts content
  Mail.deliver do
    from    my_email
    to      test_mode ? "me+#{entry[:first_name]}@gmail.com" : entry[:email]
    subject 'Thank you for your gift'
    body    content
  end
```

```
end
```

Chapter 9

9.1 Calculator

```ruby
class Calculator
  def add(a, b)
    return a + b
  end

  def minus(a, b)
    return a - b
  end
end

calc = Calculator.new
puts calc.add(2, 3)
puts calc.minus(17, calc.add(2, 3) )
```

9.2 Age of Teacher and Students

```ruby
require 'date'

class Person
  attr_accessor :name, :birth_date, :gender

  def initialize(name, b_date)
    @name = name
    @birth_date = Date.parse(b_date)
  end

  def age
    if self.birth_date
      tmp_year = Date.today.year - self.birth_date.year
      tmp_month = Date.today.month - self.birth_date.month
      tmp_day  = Date.today.day - self.birth_date.day
      return tmp_year - 1 if  (tmp_month < 0) || (tmp_month == 0  && tmp_day < 0)
      return tmp_year
```

```
    else
      nil
    end
  end

end

class Teacher < Person

end

class Student < Person
  attr_accessor :grade

  def initialize(name, b_date, grade)
    super(name, b_date)
    @grade = grade
  end

end

teacher_1 = Teacher.new("James Bond", "1968-10-23")
teacher_2 = Teacher.new("Michael Zasky", "1978-01-02")
puts "Teacher '#{teacher_1.name}' age: #{teacher_1.age}" # =>
avg_teacher_age = [teacher_1, teacher_2].collect{|y| y.age }.inject(0.0) { |result, el| r\
esult + el } / 2
puts "Average Teacher age: #{avg_teacher_age}"

students = []
students << Student.new("John Sully", "1999-10-23", 10)
students << Student.new("Michael Page", "1999-10-23", 11)
students << Student.new("Anna Boyle", "1998-12-03", 10)
students << Student.new("Dominic Chan", "1999-10-23", 10)

grade_10_students = students.select{|x| x.grade == 10}
puts "The number of Grade 10 students: #{grade_10_students.size}"
average_grade_10_age = grade_10_students.collect{|y| y.age }.inject(0.0) { |result, el| r\
esult + el } / grade_10_students.size
puts "Average Grade 10 students age: #{average_grade_10_age.round(2)}"
```

9.3 Calculate Sales Tax

```ruby
module GSTCalc
  GST_RATE = 10.0

  def net_amount
    if @sales_tax_applicable
      (@amount / (100.0 + GST_RATE) * 100.0).round(2)
    else
      return @amount
    end
  end

  def gst
    if @sales_tax_applicable
      tax = (@amount - self.net_amount).round(2)
    else
      return 0.0
    end
  end
  alias tax gst

end

class ServiceItem
  include GSTCalc

  attr_accessor :name, :amount, :sales_tax_applicable

  def self.gst_free?; return false; end

  def initialize(name, amount)
    self.name = name
    self.amount = amount
    self.sales_tax_applicable = false    # => default no sales tax
  end

end

class Goods
  include GSTCalc

  attr_accessor :name, :amount, :sales_tax_applicable

  def initialize(name, amount)
```

```
      self.name = name
      self.amount = amount
      self.sales_tax_applicable = true      # => default has sales tax
   end
end


form_roller = Goods.new("Form Roller", 49.95)
puts "#{form_roller.name} Net Amount: #{form_roller.net_amount}, GST: #{form_roller.gst}"

service_1 = ServiceItem.new("Initial Consultation", 120.0)
service_2 = ServiceItem.new("Subsequent Consultation", 80.0)
puts "#{service_1.name} Net Amount: #{service_1.net_amount}, GST: #{service_1.gst}"
puts "#{service_2.name} Net Amount: #{service_2.net_amount}, GST: #{service_2.gst}"
```

9.4 Library System

```
class Library
  @@books = []
  @@members = []
  @@rentals = []

  def self.import_books(csv_file)
    require 'csv'
    CSV.foreach(csv_file) do |row|
      next if row[0] == 'TITLE'
      a_book = Book.new
      a_book.title = row[0]
      a_book.author = row[1]
      a_book.status = "available"
      @@books << a_book
    end
  end

  def self.find_by_title(book_title)
    the_book = @@books.select{|x| x.title == book_title }.first
    if the_book.nil?
      puts "Book #{book_title} not found"
    end
    return the_book
  end

  def self.book_count
```

```ruby
      @@books.size
  end

  def self.rental_history
    @@rentals
  end

  def self.borrow(member, book)
    if book.status == "available"
      @@rentals << Rental.new(member, book)
      book.status = "checked out"
      puts "OK"
    else
      puts "The book '#{book.title}' is not available!"
    end
  end

  def self.return(book)
    the_rental = @@rentals.select{|x| x.is_active && x.book == book}.first
    book.status = "available"
    the_rental.finish
  end
end

class Book
  attr_accessor :title, :author, :status

end

class Member
  attr_accessor :name, :member_id

  def initialize(name, member_id)
    @name = name
    @member_id = member_id
  end

end

class Rental
  attr_accessor :member, :book
  attr_accessor :is_active
```

```ruby
  def initialize(member, book)
    @member = member
    @book = book
    @is_active = true
  end

  def finish
    @is_active = false
  end
end

Library.import_books(File.join(File.dirname(__FILE__), "files", "books.csv"))
Library.book_count # => 10

john = Member.new("John Sully", "1001")
mike = Member.new("Mike Zasky", "1002")

book = Library.find_by_title("Practical Web Test Automation")
Library.borrow(john, book)
Library.borrow(mike, book)
Library.return(book)
Library.borrow(mike, book)
```

9.5 Sunflower vs Zombies Simulation

```ruby
ZOMBIES_COUNT = 15
DISTANCE = 10

class Sunflower
  attr_accessor :health

  def initialize
    @health = 100
  end

  def exchange_fire(zombie)

    if zombie.in_touch_distance?
      @health -= 5
    else
      @health -= (rand(2) + 1)
    end
```

```ruby
    if @health <= 0
      @health = 0
    end

    zombie.health -= (rand(31) + 10) # between 10 to 40 damage
    if zombie.health <= 0
      zombie.die
    else
      zombie.move_forward
    end

  end

end


class Zombie
  @@live_count = 0
  attr_accessor :health, :step
  attr_accessor :moving_speed

  def initialize
    @@live_count += 1
    @health = 100
    @step = 0
    @moving_speed = rand(10) >= 8  ?  2 : 1 # 20% are jumping zombies
  end

  def self.remaining_lives
    @@live_count
  end

  def die
    @health = 0
    @@live_count -= 1
  end

  def is_dead?
    @health <= 0
  end

  def in_touch_distance?
```

```ruby
      @step == DISTANCE
    end

    def move_forward
      @step += @moving_speed
      if @step >= DISTANCE
        @step = DISTANCE
      end
    end
  end
end

print "\nY(100)  ___ ___ ___ ___ ___ ___ ___ ___ ___ ___"

sunflower = Sunflower.new
zombies = []
ZOMBIES_COUNT.times do
  zombies << Zombie.new
end

active_zombie = nil

while (sunflower.health > 0) do
  sleep 0.1  # adjust game speed, smaller number, faster

  if active_zombie.nil? || active_zombie.is_dead?
    active_zombie = zombies.shift unless zombies.empty?
  end

  break if zombies.empty? && (active_zombie.nil? || active_zombie.is_dead?) # no more zom\
bies

  sunflower.exchange_fire(active_zombie)
  flower_health_str = sunflower.health.to_s.rjust(3, " ")
  print "\r"
  print "F(#{flower_health_str})  "

  zombie_pos = "Z#{active_zombie.health.to_s.rjust(2, '0')}"
  field = 10.times.collect {|x|
    if active_zombie.step == (10-x)
      zombie_pos
    else
      "___"
    end
  }
```

```
  }.join(" ")
  print field
end

if sunflower.health > 0
  puts "\n\nYou Win! Flower survived attacks from #{ZOMBIES_COUNT} zombies"
else
  puts "\n\nGame Over! #{Zombie.remaining_lives} zombies left"
end
```

Chapter 10

10.1 Google Labs Aptitude Test

```
start_time = Time.now
(1..9).each do |w|

  (1..9).each do |d|
    next if d==w

    (0..9).each do |o|
      next if o==d || o==w

      (1..9).each do |t|
        next if t==o || t==d || t==w

        (0..9).each do |g|
          next if g==t || g==o || g==d || g==w

          (0..9).each do |l|
            next if l==g || l==t || l==o || l==d || l==w

            (0..9).each do |e|
              next if e==l || e==g || e==t || e==o || e==d || e==w

              (0..9).each do |c|
                next if c==e || c==l || c==g || c==t || c==o || c==d || c==w

                (0..9).each do |m|

                  next if m==c || m==e || m==l || m==g || m==t || m==o || m==d || m==w  \
```

```
        top_no =     w*100000 + w*10000 + w*1000 + d*100 + o*10 + t
        bottom_no = g*100000 + o*10000 + o*1000 + g*100 + l*10 + e
        result =     d*100000 + o*10000 + t*1000 + c*100 + o*10 + m

        if top_no - bottom_no == result
          puts "#{top_no} - #{bottom_no} = #{result}"
          # puts "g => #{g}, o => #{o}, l => #{l}, e => #{e}, d => #{d}, t => #\
{t}, c => #{c}, m => #{m}, w => #{w}"
        end


            end
          end
        end
      end
    end
  end
end
end

puts "Time to solve: #{Time.now - start_time}"
```

10.2 HCF (Recursion)

```
def hcf(a, b)
  if a == 0
    return b
  elsif b == 0
    return a
  else
    return hcf(b, a%b)
  end
end

puts hcf(2480, 1824)
```

10.3 Compound Interest

```ruby
def compound_interest(principal, rate, years)
  if years == 0
    return principal
  else
    principal = principal + rate * principal # new principal for this year
    return compound_interest(principal, rate, years-1)
  end
end

print "Enter deposited amount : $"
amount = gets.chomp.to_i
print "Enter interest rate (8% enter 0.08): "
rate = gets.chomp.to_f
print "For how long (years): "
years = gets.to_i
puts
the_total = compound_interest(amount, rate, years).round(2)
puts "After #{years} years, you will get $#{the_total}"
```

10.4 Farmer Crosses River Puzzle

```ruby
def is_all_crossed_river?
  @item_positions.values.all? {|x| x.to_s == "crossed"}
end

# farmer moves by himself or take another one (only one)
def move(item)
  if @item_positions[item] == :crossed
    @item_positions[:farmer] = @item_positions[item] = :not_crossed
  else
    @item_positions[:farmer] = @item_positions[item] = :crossed
  end

  @direction = @direction == :forward ? :backward : :forward
end

def undo_move(item)
  if @item_positions[item] == :crossed
    @item_positions[:farmer] = @item_positions[item] = :not_crossed
  else
    @item_positions[:farmer] = @item_positions[item] = :crossed
  end
```

```ruby
    @direction = @direction == :forward ? :backward : :forward
end


def is_safe?
  # OK if farmer is there

  items_not_crossed = @item_positions.collect{ |x, y| x if y.to_s == "not_crossed" }.comp\
act
    items_crossed = @item_positions.collect{ |x, y| x if y.to_s == "crossed" }.compact

  [items_crossed, items_not_crossed].each do |items_at_one_side|
      return false if items_at_one_side.include?(:sheep) && items_at_one_side.include?(:cab\
bage) && !items_at_one_side.include?(:farmer)
      return false if items_at_one_side.include?(:sheep) && items_at_one_side.include?(:wol\
f) && !items_at_one_side.include?(:farmer)
  end

  # false if one side wolf and sheep
  # false if one side sheep and cabbage

  return true
end

def has_done_before?
  @moving_log.values.any?{|x|
    x[:farmer] == @item_positions[:farmer] &&
    x[:sheep] == @item_positions[:sheep] &&
    x[:wolf] == @item_positions[:wolf] &&
    x[:cabbage] == @item_positions[:cabbage]
  }
end

def is_item_with_farmer?(item)
  @item_positions[item] ==  @item_positions[:farmer]
end

def print_moving_log
  @moving_log.keys.sort.each do |key|
    action_str = "Step #{key}"

    item_statuses =  @moving_log[key]
    items_not_crossed = item_statuses.collect{ |x, y| x if y.to_s == "not_crossed" }.comp\
```

```
act
    items_crossed = item_statuses.collect{ |x, y| x if y.to_s == "crossed" }.compact

    if key > 0
      prev_statuses = @moving_log[key -1]
      prev_not_crossed = prev_statuses.collect{ |x, y| x if y.to_s == "not_crossed" }.com\
pact
      prev_crossed = prev_statuses.collect{ |x, y| x if y.to_s == "crossed" }.compact

      diff_crossed = items_crossed - prev_crossed
      diff_not_crossed = items_not_crossed - prev_not_crossed

      if diff_not_crossed.empty?
        action_str += " #{diff_crossed} forward"
      else
        action_str += " #{diff_not_crossed} backward"
      end

    end
    puts action_str

    format_str = "#{items_crossed.inspect} <=  #{items_not_crossed.inspect}"
    puts format_str
  end

end

@item_positions = { :farmer => :not_crossed, :wolf => :not_crossed, :sheep => :not_crosse\
d, :cabbage => :not_crossed }
@items = [:farmer, :wolf, :sheep, :cabbage]
@step = 1
@direction = :forward
@moving_log = { 0 => @item_positions.dup } # moving log starts with all in one side

def cross

  if is_all_crossed_river?
    print_moving_log
    puts "Done!"
    return # exit out of recursion
  end

  @items.each do |item|
```

```
    next unless is_item_with_farmer?(item)
    next if item == :farmer && @direction == :forward

    move(item);

    if is_safe? && !has_done_before?
      # puts "is safe"
      # puts "#{@step}| move #{item} #{@direction}"
      @moving_log[@step] = @item_positions.dup
      # puts @item_positions.inspect

      @step += 1

      cross();  # next step, recursive

    else
      undo_move(item); # "not safe, revert"
      # puts @item_positions.inspect
    end

  end
end

cross()
```

10.5 Cryptic Math Equation (Backtracking)

```
@@letters = ['U', 'K', 'S', 'A', 'R', 'G', 'I', 'N']
@letter_to_digits = {} # hash store the solution
@is_digit_used = {0 => false, 1 => false, 2 => false, 3 => false, 4 => false, 5 => false,\
 6 => false, 7 => false, 8 => false, 9 => false }

def decode_letters_to_number(a, d)
  d.each do |k, v|
    a = a.gsub(k,v)   #if k && v
  end
  a.to_i
end

def check_ans()
  a = decode_letters_to_number('UK', @letter_to_digits)
```

```
    b = decode_letters_to_number('USA', @letter_to_digits)
    c = decode_letters_to_number('USSR', @letter_to_digits)
    d = decode_letters_to_number('AGING', @letter_to_digits)
    # puts "[DEBUG] Checking #{a} + #{b} + #{c} = #{d}"
    if a + b + c  == d
      puts "#{a} + #{b} + #{c} = #{d}" # got it
      puts @letter_to_digits
    end
  end
end

def find_out(idx = 0)
  if idx == @letters.length # got 8 letter filled
    check_ans()
    return
  end

  (0..9).each do |i|
    # assign 0 - 9 to each letter
    next if i == 0 and (@letters[idx] =='U' || @letters[idx] =='A' ) # no leading 0
    next if @letters[idx] == 'A' && i != 1
    next if @letters[idx] == 'U' && i != 9
    next if @letters[idx] == 'G' && i != 0

    unless @is_digit_used[i]
      @is_digit_used[i] = true  # the number is used
      @letter_to_digits[@letters[idx]] = i.to_s
      find_out(idx + 1)
      @is_digit_used[i] = false # clear
    end

  end
end

start_time = Time.now
find_out # start
puts "Time to solve: #{Time.now - start_time}"
```

Chapter 11

Sample Selenium Script

```
require 'selenium-webdriver'

browser = Selenium::WebDriver.for(:firefox)
browser.navigate.to("http://travel.agileway.net")

browser.find_element(:id, "username").send_keys("agileway")
browser.find_element(:id, "password").send_keys("testwise")
browser.find_element(:xpath,"//input[@value='Sign in']").click

browser.find_element(:xpath, "//input[@type='radio' and @name='tripType' and @value='onew\
ay']").click
select_elem = browser.find_element(:name, "fromPort");
options = select_elem.find_elements(:tag_name, "option");
options.each { |opt| opt.click if opt.text == "New York"}

Selenium::WebDriver::Support::Select.new(browser.find_element(:name, "toPort")).select_by\
(:text, "Sydney")
Selenium::WebDriver::Support::Select.new(browser.find_element(:id, "departDay")).select_b\
y(:text, "04")
Selenium::WebDriver::Support::Select.new(browser.find_element(:id, "departMonth")).select\
_by(:text, "March 2012")
browser.find_element(:xpath,"//input[@value='Continue']").click

browser.find_element(:name, "passengerFirstName").send_keys("Wise")
browser.find_element(:name, "passengerLastName").send_keys("Tester")
browser.find_element(:xpath,"//input[@value='Next']").click

browser.find_element(:xpath, "//input[@name='card_type' and @value='visa']").click
browser.find_element(:name, "card_number").send_keys("4000000000000000")
Selenium::WebDriver::Support::Select.new(browser.find_element(:name, "expiry_year")).sele\
ct_by(:text, "2013")
browser.find_element(:xpath,"//input[@value='Pay now']").click
```

Sample Selenium Test in RSpec

```ruby
require 'selenium-webdriver'
require 'rspec'

describe "Book flight" do

  before(:all) do
    @browser = $browser = Selenium::WebDriver.for(:firefox)
    @browser.navigate.to("http://travel.agileway.net")
  end

  after(:all) do
    @browser.quit
  end

  it "Book flight with payment" do
    @browser.find_element(:id, "username").send_keys("agileway")
    @browser.find_element(:id, "password").send_keys("testwise")
    @browser.find_element(:xpath,"//input[@value='Sign in']").click
    expect(@browser.page_source).to include("Signed in!")   # assertion

    @browser.find_element(:xpath, "//input[@type='radio' and @name='tripType' and @value=\
'oneway']").click
    Selenium::WebDriver::Support::Select.new(@browser.find_element(:name, "fromPort")).se\
lect_by(:text, "New York")
    Selenium::WebDriver::Support::Select.new(@browser.find_element(:name, "toPort")).sele\
ct_by(:text, "Sydney")
    Selenium::WebDriver::Support::Select.new(@browser.find_element(:id, "departDay")).sel\
ect_by(:text, "04")
    Selenium::WebDriver::Support::Select.new(@browser.find_element(:id, "departMonth")).s\
elect_by(:text, "March 2012")

    @browser.find_element(:xpath,"//input[@value='Continue']").click
    @browser.find_element(:name, "passengerFirstName").send_keys("Wise")
    @browser.find_element(:name, "passengerLastName").send_keys("Tester")
    @browser.find_element(:xpath,"//input[@value='Next']").click

    @browser.find_element(:xpath, "//input[@name='card_type' and @value='visa']").click
    @browser.find_element(:name, "card_number").send_keys("4000000000000000")
    select_elem = @browser.find_element(:name, "expiry_year");
    options = select_elem.find_elements(:tag_name, "option");
    options.each { |opt| opt.click if opt.text == "2013"}
    @browser.find_element(:xpath,"//input[@value='Pay now']").click
```

```
    sleep 10
    # check
    expect(@browser.page_source).to include("2012-03-04   <b>New York</b> to <b>Sydney")
  end

end
```

Resources

Solutions to exercises

http://zhimin.com/books/learn-ruby-programming-by-examples[10]

Username: `agileway`
Password: `SUPPORTWISE15`

Log in with the above, or scan QR Code to acess directly.

Code Editor

- **SciTE**[11], Windows and Linux Platform, Free.
- **TextWrangler**[12], Mac, Free.
- **TextMate**[13], Mac, 48.75 EUR.
- **Sublime Text**[14], Windows & Mac & Linux, $70.
- **Visual Studio Code**[15], Windows & Mac & Linux, Free.

Ruby Language

- **Ruby Installer for Windows**[16]

Ruby Tutorials

- **Ruby in Twenty Minutes**[17]

  Official Ruby tutorial, as its name suggests, it takes only about 20 minutes to go through.

---

[10]http://zhimin.com/books/learn-ruby-programming-by-examples
[11]http://www.scintilla.org/SciTEDownload.html
[12]http://www.barebones.com/products/textwrangler
[13]http://http://macromates.com
[14]http://www.sublimetext.com/
[15]https://code.visualstudio.com/
[16]http://rubyinstaller.org/downloads
[17]https://www.ruby-lang.org/en/documentation/quickstart

- **Codecademy's "Introduction to Ruby" course** http://www.codecademy.com[18]

  Codecademy offers free interactive coding courses. One of them is "Introduction to Ruby". Beside explaining concepts, the course also have simple exercises that you can edit and submit code.

More Exercises

- **Ruby Quiz**[19]

  A programming challenge site for Ruby programmers, contains over 150+ quizzes. The quizzes are generally quite hard.

Test Automation

- **Practical Web Test Automation**[20] by Zhimin Zhan

  A practical guide to learn and master automated testing for web applications.
- **Selenium WebDriver Recipes in Ruby**[21] by Zhimin Zhan

  Over 200 automated test solutions in Selenium WebDriver, a popular automated test framework for web applications (used in FaceBook and Google).

Others

- **Learn Swift Programming by Examples**[22] by Zhimin Zhan

  Leverage similar exercises in this book to learn a hot new programming language Swift to develop your own iOS apps.

---

[18]http://www.codecademy.com
[19]http://rubyquiz.com/
[20]https://leanpub.com/practical-web-test-automation
[21]https://leanpub.com/selenium-recipes-in-ruby
[22]https://leanpub.com/learn-swift-programming-by-examples